HEROES AND LEGENDS

SINBAD THE SAILOR

BY PHIL MASTERS

ILLUSTRATED BY aRU-MOR

ROSEN
PUBLISHING

New York

This edition published in 2016 by:
The Rosen Publishing Group, Inc.
29 East 21st Street
New York, NY 10010

Library of Congress Cataloging-in-Publication Data

Masters, Phil.
Sinbad the sailor/Phil Masters.
        pages cm.—(Heroes and legends)
Includes bibliographical references and index.
ISBN 978-1-4994-6174-9 (library bound)
[1. Fairy tales. 2. Arabs—Folklore. 3. Folklore—Arab countries.] I. Title.
PZ8.M44847Si 2015
398.2—dc23
                                2014050284

Manufactured in the United States of America

CONTENTS

INTRODUCTION: TALES WITHIN TALES

Sinbad the Sailor is one of the great travelers in world literature. He arrived in Europe at the beginning of the 18th century, and his stories became famous as part of the great *The Arabian Nights* story cycle. This was the first of many times that European readers became a bit confused about Sinbad (alias Sindbad or Es-Sindibad of the Sea). Actually, there's no real evidence that his tale formed part of *The Arabian Nights* before then. Sinbad's history is full of strange moments.

The 1,001 Nights

The Arabian Nights, also known as the *1,001 Nights*, is a collection of folktales, parables, legends, and anecdotes, set within a unifying framework. The collection seems to have come to the Arab world from Persia some time before the 10th century; its earliest origins vanish into lost history, although some scholars think that the story cycle may have originated in India. These stories would have been the repertoire of public storytellers giving performances in coffee shops and on street corners in their personal styles, so they probably changed a lot over time. The earliest surviving manuscript goes back to 14th–15th-century Syria, although there is also a very small 9th-century Egyptian fragment.

The framing story is famous. A great king discovers that his wife has been unfaithful, and, enraged at all women, resolves to avoid any more betrayals by taking a new virgin as his bride every night and having her executed in the morning. Eventually, though, Scheherazade, the daughter of his vizier, volunteers to be the next bride, tells him stories in the night, and ends them on a cliffhanger which makes him spare her so that he can hear the end of the tale. She repeats this process for 1,001 nights, even giving the king children along the way, until he announces that he will spare her completely, and they all live happily ever after.

Today, the stories of Sinbad's seven amazing voyages are often fitted into that framework. But the Sinbad stories actually have their own framework to hold them together – like that of the *The Arabian Nights*, a matter of one fictional character telling stories to another. They also have their own, obscure history, perhaps going back to ancient Egypt; they certainly include scenes that can be traced back to ancient Greek epics. However, they probably owe most of their inspiration to stories of real Arab voyages on the Indian Ocean in the 8th–10th centuries.

Arrivals in Europe

In fact, Sinbad came to Europe ahead of Scheherazade. Both were brought by a French traveler and scholar named Antoine Galland, who visited the East and then returned home to a country where local fairy tales were in fashion among well-bred readers. Around 1701, he published a French translation of the Sinbad stories. When someone then told him that they were part of a larger work, he decided that the work in question must be *The Arabian Nights*, acquired that 14th–15th-century manuscript, which still exists (at least in part) and which doesn't feature Sinbad, and published a heavily adapted French translation between 1704 and 1717. This was itself soon translated into English, although no direct English translations of any Arabic versions appeared until the 19th century.

It is actually likely that it was only after Europeans started lumping Sinbad into *The Arabian Nights* that Eastern storytellers decided that they might as well do the same. Arabic manuscripts dating from after Galland's work feature Sinbad, but there is no evidence that this was done earlier. There was certainly enough contact between East and West in the

An illustration of one of Sinbad's many monstrous encounters – in this case, with a group of giant fish. (Mary Evans Picture Library)

18th century for ideas to migrate both ways. Nor is this is the only part of *The Arabian Nights* that may have flowed back to the East from Europe. It is possible that such well-known stories as those of Aladdin and Ali Baba may have been invented by Galland, or by Middle Easterners whom he employed for advice. But both *The Arabian Nights* and the Sinbad cycle developed from the first by absorbing stories from anywhere they could be found, so all this is really just part of a continuing process.

This book tells the tale of Sinbad as it appears in modern versions of *The Arabian Nights*, and then looks at how Sinbad has moved on from there. But it all starts with his story.

THE SEVEN VOYAGES OF SINBAD

It is written that in the time of the Caliph Haroun al-Rashid, in his city of Baghdad, many wonders were seen and strange tales were told. The wealthy and powerful rubbed shoulders with the poor and unfortunate, and destiny could cast the one down and raise the other up in a moment. One tale of that age of wonder concerned a poor man and a rich man, who chanced to share a name, and who happened to meet one day.

Sinbad the Porter and Sinbad the Sailor

Among the thousands of poor men living in Baghdad was one known as Sinbad the Porter, who scraped a living carrying loads around upon his head. One hot day, he was carrying a heavy load through a wealthy part of the city when he passed the house of a merchant. The street before the house was swept and watered so there was no dust, and there was a wooden bench by the door. Sinbad the Porter felt very tired, so he stopped for a moment to mop the sweat from his brow.

As he rested, a cool breeze blew through the door, carrying a pleasant scent of fine food and wine and the sound of beautiful music and birdsong from the courtyard within. Peering through the doorway, the porter saw richly-dressed servants and slaves.

SINBAD'S NAME

Thanks to these tales, "Sinbad" is now quite a familiar name in the West, although it isn't often encountered outside stories. (It does occur in one other set of stories within *The Arabian Nights*.) Despite this association, it is probably not Arabic in origin; it seems to be Persian, or possibly Indian, and it probably means "Lord of the Sindh River." The Sindh, or Indus, is a river in what is now Pakistan, and sailors from the region were famously skilled. (Sinbad visits the region on his third voyage.) This may hint at part of the origin of the Sinbad stories.

In addition, Sinbad is called "the Sailor," which is perhaps his *laqab*, a nickname or title which often acted as something like a surname in early Arab societies. (For example, the Caliph Haroun's *laqab* was "al-Rashid," meaning "the rightly-guided.") It might be more accurate to translate Sinbad's *laqab* as "the seafarer" or "of the sea" rather than "the sailor;" in the stories, he generally leaves ship operation to professional captains, showing no special skills in that direction himself. He travels by sea a lot, but almost entirely as a merchant-passenger.

At this, Sinbad the Porter raised his eyes to heaven and gave praise to Allah. "O Creator and Provider," he said, "you bestow wealth without limit on those you favor. You make one man rich and another poor. You determine that the owner of this house shall live in comfort, while I live in poverty. None can oppose your judgement or omnipotence." And he recited verses in honor of the power of Allah.

Sinbad telling stories, as imagined by famous illustrator Gustave Doré.

Then, as he took up his load and prepared to go on his way, a page boy emerged from the house. "Come inside," said the page, "for my master wishes to speak with you."

Sinbad the Porter knew no polite way in which to refuse this invitation, so, leaving his load with the doorkeeper, he followed the page to a great hall where lords and sheiks were sitting on rich rugs among sweet-scented flowers, dining on dried fruit and other fine foods and wines, while beautiful slave girls played music and sang. At the head of the hall sat a distinguished man whose beard was touched with gray. "By Allah," thought the porter, "this is Paradise, or the dwelling of some king." So he kissed the ground respectfully, invoked a blessing upon the assembly, and stood with his head bowed.

"Come," said the master of the house, "sit by me and eat." Still knowing no way to refuse, Sinbad the Porter obeyed, wondering at the food he was offered, then washed his hands politely and thanked the company.

"Be welcome here," said his host. "Now, what is your name, and what do you do for a living?"

"My name is Sinbad," the porter replied, "and I carry loads about the city."

His host smiled. "That is a great coincidence," he said, "for my name also is Sinbad – men call me Sinbad the Sailor. Now, I would like to hear those verses I heard you recite outside my door."

"Forgive me," said Sinbad the Porter, "I live a hard life, which has taught me poor manners."

"Not at all," said Sinbad the Sailor. "Please, my brother – repeat those verses."

And so Sinbad the Porter obeyed, and Sinbad the Sailor smiled again. "I see that you wonder at my fortune," he said. "But know this, my brother – I came to this through effort, hardship, and danger. I went on seven voyages, each of which makes a tale that will astonish you. Everything was fate and the will of Allah. Rest here a while, and I will tell you my story."

Sinbad the Porter bowed his head, and Sinbad the Sailor began his telling.

The First Voyage: Living Islands and Sea Horses

It is true, said Sinbad the Sailor, that my father was one of the great men of this city, a wealthy merchant. But he died when I was young, leaving me his property. Although he had taught me something of his trade, I grew up thinking

POETRY, DESTINY, AND HOSPITALITY

This frame story shows several themes which appear in many parts of *The Arabian Nights*, being common concerns of medieval Islamic culture. If some things look a little odd to modern readers, they would have been very familiar to the original audience.

To begin with, Sinbad the Porter responds to what he sees by reciting poetry, probably from memory but perhaps actually extemporizing on the spot. This is a society with a huge respect for that art; Sinbad the Sailor and his guests are impressed by this.

Secondly, Sinbad the Porter talks about *destiny* – his own as a poor man and the very different destinies granted to the rich. Sinbad the Sailor responds by showing him how difficult and challenging his own destiny was. It's still all rather arbitrary, but it doesn't all go one way. In any case, there's no point in complaining much, as Sinbad the Porter knows; Allah is all-powerful, and mortals cannot hope to understand His plan, they can only accept it with humility. This is very much an Islamic viewpoint; human beings have free will, but Allah alone knows the future, including

what choices they will make. Fortunately, Allah is ultimately also just.

And third, Sinbad the Sailor is incredibly generous. Generosity and hospitality are much-admired virtues in this society. They are particularly important to Arabs, originally a nomadic people, because decent treatment from strangers could be a matter of life and death for a lost wanderer.

Of course, all this may well have sounded rather comforting to the poor city-dwellers who heard these stories in coffeehouses and on street corners. Their lives were poor and uncertain, but they could all dream of good luck – if not of making a fortune like Sinbad the Sailor, at least of making a good (rich) friend, as happens to Sinbad the Porter.

The professional storytellers who told these tales could recite poetry from memory, and were basically buskers whose income depended on audience donations. Stories whose morals were "poetry recitals deserve a reward" and "it's good to be generous" could have been good business for them!

nothing of that, but took possession of my inheritance and lived in ease and luxury, eating and drinking with my friends and thinking that my good fortune would last forever. By the time I realized my mistake, my inheritance was all but spent.

At first I was horrified. But then I remembered a proverb of Solomon, the son of David (peace be upon them both!), which my father had told me. "Three things are better than three other things," he said. "The day of your death is better than the day of your birth, a live dog is better than a dead lion, and the grave is better than poverty." Reflecting on this, I decided what to do.

Gathering up what was left of my moveable property and fine clothes, I sold them all, raising 3,000 silver dirhams. With that, I purchased trade goods and the wherewithal for travel, and took passage on a ship with a company of merchants, sailing from Basrah.

We sailed the ocean for many days, buying and selling wherever we landed and making good profits. Then, one day, we came to what we took for an uninhabited island, lush and beautiful as Paradise. The captain dropped anchor and put out a gangplank, and most of us went ashore. Some brought stoves so that they could make better fires than aboard ship, cooking meals and heating water so that they could wash clothes; others simply looked around.

A young Sinbad at the time of his first voyage by ªRu-Mor.

But then, suddenly, we heard a cry from the captain, who was still aboard the ship. "Save yourselves!" he called. "Quickly – leave everything! This is not an island, it is a great fish, which has floated on the surface of the sea since the creation! Sands and silt have gathered on its back, and trees have grown there, but now it feels the heat of your fires! It is already stirring, and soon it will dive beneath the waves! Flee!"

Those who had been resting leapt to their feet, and we all ran towards the ship. But the captain's warning had come too late for some. The fish dived a moment later, and we were left amidst a chaos of cooking pots and stoves. The captain, struggling to save his ship, did not look back; as I was engulfed by the waves, I watched him sail away.

But by great good fortune, I was able to keep my head above water, and after a moment a wooden washtub floated past me. I grasped it, and so I stayed afloat even as everyone else drowned.

ISLAND MONSTERS

Sinbad's encounter with an "island" that is actually a sea monster isn't unique in mythology. Similarly confusing creatures appear in Greek bestiaries (the *aspidochelone*, a giant turtle), in Anglo-Saxon manuscripts (a whale named "Fastitocalon"), and in the Renaissance Italian epic *Orlando Furioso*. In the medieval Irish *Navigation of St. Brendan*, the saint and his crew of monks encounter a giant fish named "Jasconye" in the middle of the Atlantic, and make much the same mistake as Sinbad and his colleagues, though all the monks in that story survive. A 9th-century Arab writer called this creature the *zaratan*; a 13th-century Persian, thought that some sea turtles were big enough to inspire the mistake.

This story may well have arisen independently more than once, perhaps inspired by sailors' stories of whales. Accounts of creatures that were big enough to mistake for rock outcrops at first glance doubtless grew in the telling, and the image of sailors running for their lives as the "island" shifts beneath them would have been too good to pass up. The *aspidochelone* was also explicitly a metaphor for Satan; a monstrous being who deliberately deceived humans whom he wanted to devour.

Sinbad was not the only legendary seafarer to mistake a giant fish for an island. Here, a medieval Irish monk, St. Brendan, has a similar encounter in the Atlantic. (Mary Evans Picture Library)

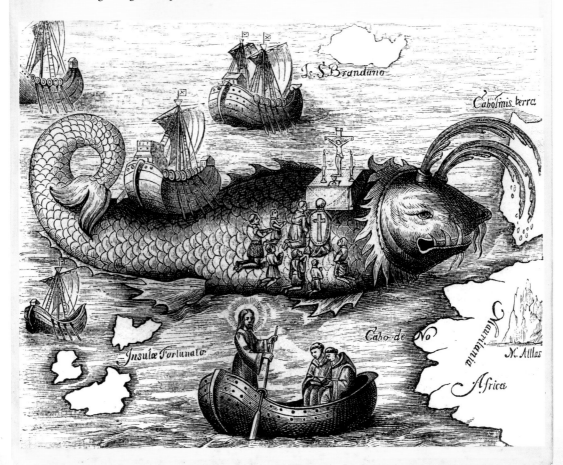

I floated alone, holding onto the washtub, for a night and a day, but my luck held, as wind and currents carried me to another island. The shore there was steep and high, but there were trees growing down to the edge, with branches hanging over the water, and I grasped hold of one, and hauled myself out. Only then did I realize that I had lost all feeling in my legs, and indeed fish had been nibbling the very flesh of my feet.

And so I collapsed, unable to move, and fell asleep where I lay. The next morning I awoke, however, with just enough strength to look around, and discovered that the island had trees bearing edible fruit and many fresh-water springs. Thus, gradually, I regained my strength. After a few days, I made myself a staff from a tree branch, and was able to explore a little more.

So it was that, one day, I saw something new in the distance, which at first I took for a wild animal. Approaching closely, though, I saw that it was a horse, a fine mare, tethered by the shore. As I approached it in puzzlement, it saw me coming and let out a loud, shrill neigh. Startled and unnerved by this, I turned to retreat.

Then, however, a man suddenly appeared, emerging from a hiding place in the ground nearby and calling "Who are you and how came you here?"

"Sir," I replied, "my name is Sinbad, and I am a stranger in this land. I was traveling on a ship when I was cast into the sea, and the waves brought me here."

At that, he became sympathetic. "Come with me," he said, taking me by the arm, and led me back to his hiding place. This was an underground chamber, where he sat me down and gave me food and drink. In return, I told him my full story. "But please, by Allah, tell me," I said when I had finished, "who are you, and why are you hiding, and why is that mare tethered by the sea?"

"Well," my host said, "I am one of several men stationed here. We are the grooms of King Mihrajan, who rules this island, and tonight is the night of the new moon. On this night, the wonderful sea-horse will emerge from the waves onto this shore. That is why we bring virgin mares from our stables here. The sea-horse is a stallion, and when he catches their scent, he will come and mount one of them. Then he will try to take his new mate back under the waves, but we tether the mares firmly. So the stallion will grow angry and batter the mare with his head and hooves. When we hear him, we will drive him off. Then, in due course, the mare will give birth to as fine a foal as any you have seen, worth a fortune."

"But anyway," he went on, "when this business is done, I will take you to my master, and show you the country. It is lucky for you that we met, for otherwise you would doubtless have perished alone here."

Then, as we talked, a great stallion did indeed emerge from the sea, and mounted the mare near to us. Everything happened as I had been told, and when the stallion began to batter the mare, my new friend took up a sword and shield, and ran out to drive it off. The other grooms too emerged, waving spears and shouting, and the sea-horse fled.

(OVERLEAF)
This picture shows the ship on which Sinbad has been traveling making its narrow escape when the giant fish awakens and dives, leaving Sinbad struggling unnoticed in the water among assorted flotsam, including the washtub which he will use to stay afloat. The "fish" is described in some versions of the story as a whale, and some accounts of island monsters actually talk about giant turtles, but this depiction is based partly on medieval depictions of sea monsters and partly on large fish such as the barracuda.

The ship in the picture is based on attempted modern reconstructions of Arab trading dhows from the Abbasid period, although there is some debate about the date of introduction of features such as the triangular sails now considered characteristic of the type.

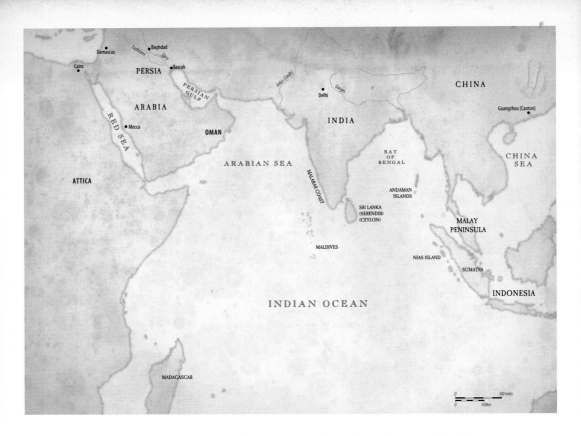

A map of the Indian Ocean and its environs, as mythologized to become the scene of Sinbad's adventures, with identifiable locations from the stories marked.

Then the other grooms gathered round me, and I told my story again. Afterwards, they untethered and saddled all the mares, so that we could ride one each. They showed me the way across the island to the city of King Mihrajan. There, they led me before the king, and I saluted him respectfully and told my tale once more.

"Fate has indeed favored you," said the king. "Allah be praised for your survival!" And from then on, he treated me with courtesy, making me a part of his court. Soon, because of my experience in trade, he made me his agent in the port. He gave me robes of honor, and I was able to intercede with him on behalf of his subjects, and so become popular.

When I spoke with merchants in the port, I made a point of asking about Baghdad and Basrah, but none ever seemed to know of my homeland. However, I heard and saw more wonders in that region than I could ever tell.

Then, one day, a ship like many others, but somehow familiar to me, sailed in, and the merchants on board came ashore. I recorded the goods they were carrying, then asked if they had anything else.

"Yes," said the captain, "we have property in the hold that belonged to another merchant who was traveling with us, but who was drowned. We intend to sell it and reserve the money, to give to his family when we return to our home city."

"What was his name?" I asked.

"He was called Sinbad," said the captain.

At that, I looked at him closely and realized that this was indeed the captain I knew, though he had been burned by the sun and weathered by hardship. "By Allah!" I cried, "This is a wonder, for I am that Sinbad!"

The captain scowled. "There is no strength save in Allah," he declared, "and no trust among men. You are trying to take our companion's property for yourself! We saw him drown, along with others, none of whom were saved, and now you dare to pretend to be him!"

I realized that I had been even more changed by time and circumstance than him. And so I drew breath, and told him the tale of how I had survived the giant fish. I reminded him of all that had passed between us after we left Baghdad, and listed what was among my goods.

"By Allah, this is a wonder indeed!" the captain declared, and called to the other travelers. I repeated my tale yet again, and they embraced me as one returned from the dead. Then I went into the hold of the ship, and found all my goods, safe and intact. Drawing some fine items from my stock, I took my old friends up to the palace, told King Mihrajan what had happened and then presented him with the goods as a gift. He was pleased at all this and gave me gifts of great value in return.

A modern Arab dhow. The basic design of these sailing vessels may not have changed much since Abbasid times. (© Marion Kaplan / Alamy)

"And now," I said to him, "I ask your permission to depart, for I yearn to see my home again."

The king was sorry at this, for he had a great affection for me, but he honored my wishes and gave me permission to depart. So I sold my trade stock in his city for a great profit, bought more goods, and boarded the ship. We set sail back to Basrah, where I rested a while, rejoicing to have survived the ocean. Then I traveled up to Baghdad, and returned to my family home. I sold all the goods I had acquired on my voyage, regaining a great fortune, and acquired servants and concubines and more fine houses. For a time, then, I lived once again for comfort and pleasure, eating and carousing with my friends and forgetting the hardships of my first voyage.

Thus it was that I was tempted to take once more to the seas ... But that is a tale for the morrow, if you wish to hear it.

At that, Sinbad the Porter gave thanks to his host, saying that he would indeed return, Allah willing. Sinbad the Sailor gave him a gift of a hundred gold dinars to take away, and he returned to his humble home and spent the night meditating upon the wondrous story which he had heard.

Sinbad and the giant serpents. During his journey through the Diamond Mountains, Sinbad has to hide in terror from the local wildlife.

The Second Voyage: The Flight of the Roc

The next morning, Sinbad the Porter rose early and went to the house of Sinbad the Sailor, who greeted him warmly and sat him down with food and drink. More guests arrived, and when all were seated, Sinbad the Sailor began his next tale.

As I have told you, after my first voyage, I was living in comfort here in Baghdad, he said. Thus it was that I forgot the hardships of travel, and remembered only the strange and wonderful sights and the profits I had made. I was drawn once more to the sea.

And so I took some of my fortune and spent it on a stock of trade goods. Then I sailed down to Basrah, where I found a fine, newly-built ship at the docks, with a stout crew. I joined the party of merchants aboard, and we set sail the same day.

We traveled from land to land, trading profitably everywhere. Then, one day, we came to an island that we saw was lush and hospitable, with fresh springs and birds singing sweetly in the branches of fruit trees, but no inhabitants. The captain ordered the anchor dropped, and many of us went ashore to rest and refresh ourselves and to give thanks to Allah for creating this place.

I myself set out to explore, carrying a little food with me. Eventually, I came to a sweet spring of clear water, where I sat down to eat. A soft breeze was blowing, and soon I lay back and went to sleep.

When I awoke, the island was quieter than ever; looking around, I could not see or hear a soul. I hurried back to the beach, and saw nothing there but the distant whiteness of the ship's sail on the horizon. It had departed without anyone giving me a thought.

At once, I berated myself for my folly. I had been living in comfort and ease, but now, thanks to my restlessness, I was once again alone on a deserted island. "The jug does not always remain unbroken," I told myself. "Last time, I was lucky, but now I will surely die alone!"

But even when I was done weeping, I could not remain still. I searched the island once again, and decided to climb a tree for a better view. At first I saw nothing but the green leaves of other trees and the blue sea, but then I caught a glimpse of something white in the distance that might have been a building.

And so I descended and hastened that way, coming in time to what seemed to be a vast white dome made of some hard material. I found no signs of windows or doors, and discovered that it was a full 50 paces in circumference.

As I puzzled over this, darkness suddenly fell upon me. I looked up and was astonished, for what I had taken for a cloud was actually a gigantic bird, descending towards me!

Then I remembered travelers' tales of the roc, a bird so huge that it preys upon elephants, carrying them off to feed to its young. I realized that what

A roc returns to its nest as night falls, watched cautiously by Sinbad.

On his second voyage, Sinbad escapes after being marooned on a remote island by tying himself to the leg of a roc, a gigantic bird, using his turban cloth to improvise a rope for the purpose. Although the bird eventually lands in an uninhabited and monster-infested mountain valley, it is shown here flying over a region with a few buildings – possibly old ruins. One of the giant serpents which infest the region can also be seen down on the mountain slopes.

Some descriptions of the roc, though not this story, claim that it is all white in color, which would fit a bird that, like a gull or an albatross, frequently flies over open ocean. However, this depiction is based on the African fish eagle (also known as the African sea eagle), which can be encountered flying over the Indian Ocean, where Sinbad sailed. This, like the roc, is a capable large predator, and does have a white head, neck, and tail.

I had thought to be a dome could only be an egg, half-buried in the soft ground. I huddled down in fear, but I was too small for the roc to notice; it settled down on its nest, stretched its legs out behind it, and went to sleep as night fell.

Now I saw a chance of escape from this island. Removing my turban, I stretched and twisted the fabric to make a rope, and used that to lash myself to the roc's leg. Then I spent a restless night.

In the morning, the roc awoke and, giving a great cry, sprang into the air, with me still tied to its leg. It soared higher and higher, until it almost reached the heavens beyond the sky. Then it began to descend, rushing down to land on a high ridge. I quickly untied myself, giving thanks that the bird had never noticed me, and hid behind a boulder. Meanwhile, the roc picked up something from the ground in its talons and once more took flight. Staring after it, I saw that it was carrying off a gigantic serpent, large enough to provide it with a meal.

When it was gone, I looked around and saw that the ridge was at the head of a deep, barren, rugged valley, which was surrounded on all sides by mountains so tall that I could not see their peaks. Now I realized that my situation might be even worse than before. On the island, at least there had been fresh water and fruit!

But I resolved that I should at least explore further, and set out down the valley. The ground felt strange beneath my feet, and I was startled to realize that it was made entirely of diamond, the stone so hard that it can be used to drill into other gemstones and porcelain. Then, looking around some more, I discovered that the valley was in fact infested with more of the gigantic serpents, larger than palm trees, big enough to devour elephants. As night began to fall, I realized that they had to remain hidden during the day for fear of the rocs, but came out at night to feed. Hence, I needed shelter for the night.

Looking round, I found a cave, with a boulder nearby that I could roll over the entrance. I stepped inside and moved the boulder. However, just as I began to relax, my eyes became accustomed to the darkness, and I saw at the far end of the cave one of the giant serpents – a mother, wrapped around a clutch of eggs!

But I had no option now but to stay quietly where I was. I spent a sleepless night thus, terrified lest the monster notice me. I was relieved beyond measure when morning came and the other serpents returned to their lairs. Carefully, I rolled the boulder back and ventured out once more.

As I made my way along, I was startled when suddenly I saw something tumbling down the slopes nearby. I was even more surprised to see that it was the carcass of a whole sheep, slaughtered and skinned, though there were no people or creatures around.

Then I remembered a story I had heard from other travelers, of the lands of the Diamond Mountains. The valley where diamonds were found was, I had been told, completely inaccessible, and so the traders of those lands had invented a way to retrieve the stones. They took sheep and slaughtered and skinned them, and threw the carcasses down into the valley from the heights of a nearby mountain. Because they were fresh, soft, and bloody, some of the diamonds would stick to them. The great vultures and eagles of the region would be drawn to the meat, descend into the valley, take up the carcasses, and fly up to their nests in the heights to feed. Then, the diamond traders would drive off the birds, recover the carcasses, and gather the diamonds that were stuck to them.

Obviously, this was that very valley. As soon as I realized this, I formed a plan. I looked around and gathered up as many large diamonds as I could, filling my pockets and the folds of my garments. Then I removed my turban and once again twisted it into a rope. As I was doing so, another carcass came tumbling down, and I used my turban to lash myself to that, lying flat on the ground underneath it.

After just a moment, I felt something grasp the carcass. One of the eagles had indeed picked it up, and I was carried up to the heights. There, the bird was about to begin feasting when I heard a loud shout and the banging of a stick against rocks. The bird took flight, and I unfastened myself and stood beside the carcass, covered in its gore.

The man who had made the noise came running up, stick in hand, but stopped with fear on his face when he saw me. However, although he knew not what to make of me, he still examined the carcass. But he found no diamonds,

THE LEGENDARY ROC

The roc, or rukh, is a giant bird which features in a number of Arabian tales and accounts, but is best known for its appearance in the Sinbad stories. Some scholars identify it with the Simurgh of Persian mythology, or even with Garuda in Indian legends; both were also big enough to carry off elephants. But Garuda was more or less a god, while the Simurgh was the king (or maybe queen) of the birds, with intelligence, speech, and mystical powers. The roc, although vengeful and clever, is basically just a very big bird.

The legend may simply have originated with travelers' tales of large eagles or vultures which grew in the telling. Another theory is that seafarers saw flightless ostriches in Africa and decided that they must be the chicks of a *really* big species, but the snag with that is that the ostrich used to be found in Arabia, so Arabians would have been familiar with it. Stories of the now-extinct flightless "elephant bird" of Madagascar, or of its eggs, may also have been involved; that was even bigger than the ostrich. Although Sinbad doesn't mention the fact, some accounts say that the roc was white in color, which is something perhaps associated most with sea-birds.

As well as mentioning stories that the roc came from Madagascar, the great Italian traveler Marco Polo said that envoys from China presented the Mongol ruler Kublai Khan with a roc feather. This, and the roc quills occasionally mentioned in other accounts, may actually have been raffia palm fronds, which do look quite like feathers from a really big bird.

One of the most popular incidents in the stories, among readers and illustrators, is when Sinbad ties himself to the roc's leg and is carried through the sky.

because I had moved it before any could become stuck to it. So the man set up a lamentation, complaining that evil fate had deprived him of his fortune.

Then I approached him, and he remembered me and looked at me again with trepidation, maybe taking me for a demon. "What are you?" he demanded.

"Have no fear," I replied. "I am a civilized man like yourself. I have a strange tale to tell, of how I passed through that valley. I have brought diamonds from among the serpents and I can give you more than enough to make your fortune."

Hearing that, the trader called down blessings upon me and we began to talk. As we did so, others of his party came up, each of whom had thrown a sheep down into the valley. So I told them all my story and they congratulated me. "Allah has granted you a second life," they said, "no man before has escaped from among the serpents."

Then I gave the first man some of the diamonds that I was carrying, and he and his friends took me back to their camp, where we spent the night. The next day, I traveled on with them, down to a seashore where a boat was waiting which carried us to a great and verdant island. This was covered in giant camphor trees and herds of a strange sort of buffalo roamed the land, along with a giant animal named the rhinoceros, which has a single great horn 20 feet (6 m) long. I was told that this beast sometimes slays elephants, and can then continue to walk about unconcerned with the victim skewered on that horn until the sun makes grease from the corpse melt and run down the horn, blinding the rhinoceros. Then it too dies, and the roc comes along and carries both bodies off.

In a town on that island, I sold more of my diamonds. Then I sailed off once again with my new friends. We sailed from land to land until we reached Basrah, from which traveled back home to Baghdad, where I sold the last of my diamonds and trade goods for a great profit.

Then I settled down once again, wearing fine clothes, eating good food, and drinking fine wine, until again a foolish wanderlust overcame me ... But I will tell the story of my third voyage tomorrow.

At that, Sinbad the Porter thanked his host for the wonderful tale, and Sinbad the Sailor gave him another gift of a hundred dinars before he returned home.

The Third Voyage: Evil Apes and Man-Eating Giants

The next day, after a night dreaming of giant birds and serpents, Sinbad the Porter arose, said his prayers, and went to the house of Sinbad the Sailor. His host greeted him, gave him food and drink, and, when more friends had arrived, began to talk.

As I said, even after the hardships of my first two voyages, my foolish soul was full of the desire to see new things and of the greed for profit. And so, in time, I once again used some of my fortune to buy trade goods, and ventured down to Basrah. There, I found a large ship with a good crew and several other merchants already aboard, so I joined that company.

We sailed for some time, trading wherever we went and admiring the wonders of Allah's creation. But then, one day, as we were running before a strong wind which was whipping up the waves, we heard the captain, who was on deck nd scanning the horizons, burst into cries of lamentation. When we crowded around him, we saw him rend his clothes and pluck his beard in despair.

"We are lost!" he declared. "This wind has driven us to the Island of the Hairy Ones! No one ever escapes from those creatures!"

SAVAGE ISLANDS

The land of savage, dwarfish apes and monstrous giants that appears in the story of Sinbad's third voyage is not the only island with dangerous inhabitants that Sinbad visits. During his fourth voyage, he meets a cannibal island tribe; in the alternative account of his seventh voyage, he meets piratical locals on the high seas, and is sold into slavery on a nearby island. Such tales doubtless originated with Arabian voyagers on the medieval Indian Ocean, who would have met a fair number of pirates and suspicious natives.

For example, according to Arab geographers, the inhabitants of the Andaman Islands, in the Bay of Bengal, were savage cannibals given to eating captured victims alive. In fact, the Andaman Islanders, members of an isolated ethnic group, were often violently hostile to foreign visitors (and one or two surviving tribes are still very cautious), but there is no good evidence of cannibalism.

Likewise, some expeditions would have skirted the northern coasts of Sumatra, whose inhabitants included the Batak people, who definitely did engage in ritual cannibalism. The idea of those cannibals met by Sinbad who fed their victims stupefying drugs before fattening them for slaughter may have come from the fact that hashish used to be employed as a spice in cooking in that part of the world. Further south, the inhabitants of Nias Island, west of Sumatra, long retained a formidable warrior culture and sometimes engaged in head-hunting; Arab travelers also reported cannibalism.

And indeed, we saw that we were being driven towards an island that rose steeply and stark from the sea. Bare moments later, a horde of Hairy Ones came swarming like locusts, swimming out and surrounding the ship. They were hideous creatures, more like apes than men, barely three feet tall and covered in thick black fur, with glittering yellow eyes. They chittered among themselves, but the captain said that they never had dealings with men, so no one could learn to speak with them.

They clambered aboard the ship and we dared not fight them because it was certain that they could tear us apart by weight of numbers if they chose. They bit through our anchor cables and ropes with their sharp teeth, so that we could not control the ship, which quickly went aground on the island. Then they lifted us all up bodily and threw us ashore, then swarmed back to the ship and somehow took control of it, sailing it away we knew not where.

We had no choice but to see what there was on the island, and at least we soon found fruit trees, edible herbs, and a fresh spring. Then, looking further, we saw a building. It was a gigantic castle of dark stone, with double gates of ebony hanging open. Venturing inside, we found a central courtyard that seemed deserted, although we never found any entrance to the rest of the building. On one side was a heap of bones. At the far end we saw a vast stone bench and an open oven. By the side of the oven were a stack of logs, all larger than a man and a number of huge iron roasting spits. Above it hung an array of copper cooking pots.

Exhausted by our ordeal and knowing not what more to do, for we had seen all there seemed to be on the island, we slumped down in the courtyard,

Sinbad's tale of the man-eating giant seems to derive from the Greek legend of Odysseus and a one-eyed cyclops. Hence, some illustrations, such as this one, show the giant with one eye, although the story doesn't support this.

the closest available thing to shelter, and fell into unhappy sleep. As darkness fell, though, we were all awakened by a noise like thunder that shook the ground beneath us. Looking up, we saw a vast figure scrambling down the outside of the castle. It was a giant in the shape of a man, but tall as a full-grown palm tree, jet black in color with eyes like burning red sparks. It had a mouth like a dark well with teeth like a wild boar's tusks, flapping lips like those of a camel hanging down to its chest, ears like boats hanging down to its shoulders, and fingernails like a lion's claws.

When this monster cast its gaze on us, we were paralysed with terror. It reached the ground, entered the courtyard, closed the double gates behind it, and sat for a few moments on the bench, contemplating us. Then it rose to its feet and came over to us. Suddenly, it reached out, grabbed my hand, and lifted me off the ground. It prodded and poked me all over with its fingers, and I felt that I was being examined as if by a butcher. But I had been left thin and wiry by travel and physical work, and it cast me aside. It did the same to several of my companions, until it came to the captain. He was a broad-shouldered stocky man, and the giant gave a horrible smile as it examined him.

It threw him on the ground and put its foot on his neck, breaking it. Then it took up one of the iron spits and thrust it through the poor man from mouth to backside. After that, it lit a fire in the oven and proceeded to roast the captain whole. When he was cooked, it took his body, tore it apart, and ate it as a man might eat a roast chicken. Then it lay down on the bench and went to sleep, snorting and snoring as we cowered in terror.

The next morning, the giant rose and departed, leaving us shivering in fear. "By Allah," we cried to each other, "better to have drowned, or to have been killed by the apes, than to be cooked and eaten!" Once we were sure that the giant was gone for the time being, we ventured out of the ebony gates and spent the whole day searching the island for somewhere to hide. But there was nowhere.

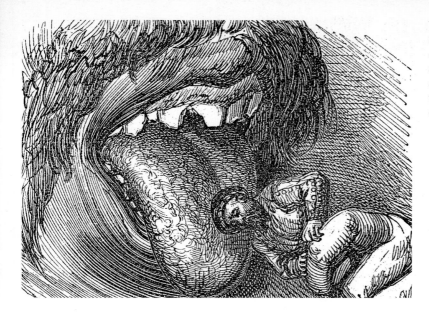

The giant met by Sinbad
and his companions
during his third voyage is
an enthusiastic man-eater,
although the story suggests
that it prefers its food
cooked.

So it was that when night began to fall, and the cold winds began to beat on us, we wandered back to the poor shelter of the castle, wondering if the giant would return. Terror made us feeble, and we feared what it would do if it had to chase us. But our fears were realized; at sunset, we heard the sound like thunder, and the giant descended on us once again. It snatched up one of the merchants and killed, roasted, and ate him, then fell asleep again on the bench.

The next morning, when the giant was gone, we gathered our wits and talked of our plight. "Better to throw ourselves in the sea and drown than to suffer this ghastly death," said one of my companions. "Listen!" said another, "We must kill this monster! Such evil does not belong in the world!"

All agreed with this, and then I spoke. "Then let us build a raft," I said, "so that we may escape this island once we have done our best to stop this evil. If we are lucky, we may reach another island. If we are unlucky, we will drown, but at least we will die struggling against evil."

The others approved of this, so we spent the day dragging some of the logs from the giant's firewood stack down to the shore. We lashed them together into a raft, which we loaded with such food and drink as we could muster. Then we retreated back to the shelter of the courtyard.

When night fell, all went as before; the giant descended on us, snatched up the stoutest of my companions, killed, cooked, and ate him, and then fell asleep. Then, when we were sure that it was unconscious, we crept out from the corner of the courtyard and set to work. We took up two of the iron spits and pushed them deep into the fire that was still burning in the oven. When they were glowing red, we formed two groups, pulled both spits from the fire, and moved as quietly as we could over to the monster.

(OVERLEAF)
On his third voyage, a
shipwrecked Sinbad and his
companions are exploring a
huge palace when they are
captured by a hideous giant
– a man-eating monster
which roasts its victims on
great iron spits. After several
of them have been killed and
eaten, the travelers escape
after blinding the giant with
a pair of its own spits, which
they first make red hot in the
cooking fire.
   By his own account,
Sinbad, now an experienced
adventurer, takes charge
during this incident.
Stealth is essential; only by
attacking unexpectedly
and simultaneously are the
humans able to blind the
giant and make any kind of
escape from the island.

This depiction of the man-eating giant by ªRu-Mor is much more faithful to the story.

Then, on a signal, we stabbed the spits as hard as we could, deep into the giant's two eyes, putting all our weight behind them.

But so huge was the monster that we did not pierce its brain, and so full of unholy vitality that even this did not kill it. It gave a horrifying cry and leapt to its feet, casting the spits aside as we were thrown back. We had completely blinded it, though, and it began to blunder around, waving its hands as we ducked and dodged. Then, groaning in agony, it felt its way to the ebony gates, pushed them open, and lurched away into the night.

We took our opportunity, and followed it through the gates. We ran down to the beach, pushed the raft out onto the waves, clambered aboard, and began paddling as best we could.

But behind us we heard a bestial roar and, looking back, we saw the giant returning. It was being guided by another of its own kind, a she-giant hideous as itself. She saw us and, howling curses in their monstrous language, she brought the male down to the shore. We were out to sea by then, and the giants had no taste for swimming. But instead, the giantess helped the male as they both picked up huge rocks, and then guided his arm as both of them began to hurl the boulders at us.

Fortunately, with the darkness and the distance, neither of them hit our raft square on. But the rocks were so huge that any which landed in the sea nearby swamped us, and one swept over us, killing several of my companions in one blow. By the time that we had paddled out of their range, all but three of us were dead.

SINBAD AND ODYSSEUS

Anyone who knows their classics will find the man-eating giant encountered by Sinbad during his third voyage, and the means by which it is escaped, more than a little familiar. In Homer's *Odyssey*, a tale of a legendary voyager from Bronze Age Greece, Odysseus and his men meet a cyclops, a one-eyed giant named Polyphemus, who traps them in his cave and eats several of them. Odysseus offers Polyphemus some strong wine, and Polyphemus promises him a gift in exchange for his name. Odysseus says that his name is "Nobody," and Polyphemus says that his gift will be that Odysseus will be eaten last. But Polyphemus then falls into a drunken sleep, and Odysseus and his men fire-harden a sharp stake in the fire and plunge it into the monster's eye. When Polyphemus calls for help, his fellow cyclopes ask who has hurt him, and laugh when Polyphemus says "Nobody."

The next morning, Polyphemus lets his sheep out to graze, sitting in the cave mouth and feeling their backs to make sure that the humans aren't slipping out with them. But Odysseus and his men tie themselves under the sheep, and so escape to their ship. However, Odysseus cannot resist taunting the giant, who hurls huge rocks towards the sound of his voice, nearly sinking the ship.

Other, fainter echoes of Homer, and of other classical tales, also appear in Sinbad's stories; for example, the crewmen drugged by cannibals might recall Odysseus's encounter with the lotus-eaters, while a predecessor of the roc appears in the Roman writer Lucian's *True History*. But this doesn't prove systematic borrowing; some story ideas just occur to more than one writer.

The medieval Arabs certainly knew about Homer; they had libraries full of classical literature. However, nobody translated the *Odyssey* into Arabic until the 20th century, and academic scholars of Greek were very different people from the storytellers who shaped the Sinbad cycle. It's more likely that Homer's story survived in the oral tradition of the eastern Mediterranean, merging with Arab folktales. A similar tale of a one-eyed man-eating giant who is blinded and then slain by a hero certainly also appears in Turkish legends.

Unfortunately, it is very hard to guess exactly how the oral tradition worked across thousands of years and multiple languages, so the relationship between these stories may remain forever a mystery. Still, Sinbad and Odysseus, lost sailors facing monsters and the whims of fate, are definitely both part of a grand tradition.

The Greek legend of Odysseus and the cyclops, as depicted here, may have inspired events in the tale of Sinbad's third voyage. (© The Art Archive / Alamy)

We three were now safe from the giants, but adrift on the ocean. We drifted for a full day and a night, until fortune brought us to another island and cast us up on the shore. There, exhausted by our ordeal, my two companions and I staggered up the beach and then fell and slept where we lay.

Barely had night come, however, when we awoke again. We were aghast to see that, as we slept, a gigantic snake had coiled its body around us. Before we could act, it saw us move and reacted by snatching one of my companions with its jaws. It swallowed him, first up to the shoulders and then entirely, and we heard his bones crack in its belly. Then it slithered away into the lush undergrowth nearby.

My surviving companion and I looked at each other in horror, and we bemoaned the fate that carried us from one terrible death to another. But the snake was gone and it was dark. Thus, we had no choice but to sleep where we lay again. When dawn came, we lived still, and we set out to explore the island.

We found fruit to eat and a spring from which to drink. We guessed that the snake would return, and so, as the day came to an end, we sought out the tallest tree on the island, hoping that this might give us safety.

We scrambled up it and settled as best we could among the highest branches. But come nightfall, our worst fears came true. The snake came slithering, tracking us we knew not how, and, when it came to the tree, it coiled round the trunk and climbed up with ease.

I had reached a higher branch than my companion, and so it reached him first. It plucked him from the tree and swallowed him whole, and again I heard his bones break. Then it slipped down the tree and vanished away.

The next day I descended once more to the ground, despairing of my fate. I considered casting myself into the sea, to put an end to this tale of horrors, but I could not do so. Life is terribly precious to us, even at such times.

Then, looking at the remnants of the raft that had brought us to the island, lashed together with improvised ropes, I formed a desperate plan. After I had eaten and drunk, as the sun sank in the west, I gathered together five strong pieces of wood, and whatever cords and ropes I could locate. I lashed one wooden beam crosswise to my ankles, so that it projected to either side of me. Then I took three more pieces, and tied them against me, one on my left side, one on my right, and one against my chest. Then, finally, I took the last wooden beam and tied it crosswise over my shoulders, projecting outwards there. Then I drew my hands and head within this improvised wooden cage as best I could, and lay shivering.

I did not have long to wait. Again, with darkness came the snake. It slithered up to me and attempted to devour me as it had my companions. But it could not! The wooden bars were long and strong enough, and I had tied them so that they braced each other. The monster's throat was not large enough for it to swallow the crosswise beams, and when it tried to batter or crush me, the bars around me held.

The snake was enraged. It thrashed and hissed in frustration, but at length, it slithered away in search of other prey.

And so I lay for the night in my cage, giving thanks to Allah. When the sun rose, I carefully untied the beams, put them aside, and once more set out to look for fruit and water.

Then, as I wandered along the beach, I saw something far out to sea. It was a ship! Instantly, I gathered up the largest branch that I could find, began to wave it, and shouted myself hoarse.

Again, I was fortunate. The crew of the ship saw the movement and turned to find out more. When they saw that I was a man, they sent a boat ashore and brought me to their vessel. Once aboard, I found that this was a large trading ship, carrying many merchants.

They were good folk, and they gave me food and drink, as well as clothes to replace the rags that were all that I had left now. I thanked them and gave thanks to Allah for my salvation. Not long afterwards, the ship came to an inhabited land called Salahita Island, where it dropped anchor, and the merchants went ashore to trade. Then, the captain turned to me.

"Listen, my friend," he said, "you say that you are a merchant who has lost everything. Would you perform a task for us, for fair pay, so you can afford to travel back to your home?"

"Gladly," I said.

"There was a merchant traveling with us before who was lost," the captain explained. "We still have his goods. We know not whether he lives or is dead, but it would surely be fairest if we sold those goods and returned the money to him, or to his family – whatever we find when we seek him in Baghdad, his home. His stock should fetch good prices here. I ask you to deal with this, in return for a broker's commission."

"That is fair," I said.

And so I went with the captain to move the lost merchant's goods from the hold to the dock. When they were being carried ashore, a clerk asked in whose name they should be registered.

"Write that they are the property of Sinbad the Sailor, being sold on his behalf," said the captain. I gasped as the clerk nodded, but restrained myself from saying anything immediately. But I looked about me, and saw that much about the ship was familiar, now that I looked with rested eyes and disregarded recent repairs and new sails.

And so I waited until the goods were safely offloaded and the merchants were discussing business. Only then did I turn once more to the captain. "Sir," I said, "what did you know of the man whose goods you have charged me to sell?"

"Little," said the captain. "He traveled with this ship on its very first voyage, when we set sail from Basrah. But I never came to know him myself before he was lost on an uninhabited island. I should have dealt with his goods long since."

"No matter," I said, "for you know him now. I am that Sinbad the Sailor whom you left by accident on that island!" And then I told him what had befallen me from that time on.

The captain was startled by this, and the other merchants gathered around, some believing, some holding me to be a joker or a fraud. But then, as I told of my adventure among the Diamond Mountains, one of them, to whom I had not spoken before, gave a cry.

"Can this be true?" he asked, pushing forward through the crowd. As he drew close, I looked at him, and saw that his face was familiar. "Yes," he said,

Arguably the most popular movie version of the legend, *The Golden Voyage of Sinbad* (1973) starred John Phillip Law as the swashbuckling Sinbad, seen here with Caroline Munro as the slave girl. (© INTERFOTO / Alamy)

"I know this man." He turned to the others. "You remember," he said, "I have told you of the time when I visited that valley, and threw a sheep carcass in. And you remember, do you not, that I told you how, when the scavenger bird brought the carcass back up, there was a man clinging to it?"

"Yes," said the others, "and we still do not believe you."

"Believe me now," said the merchant. "For this is the very same man, Sinbad the Sailor. He also told me of his previous adventures. I owe him much, for he gave me great diamonds from the valley, before we traveled to Basrah together. We parted company there, for he was returning to Baghdad. But now he is before me once again."

At this, everyone was cast into confusion and wonder. At length, the captain spoke to me, asking about the mark I had placed on my bales of goods. I described it, and also reminded him of events that had taken place on his ship when first it sailed. At that, all agreed that I was telling the truth.

And so my goods were returned to me, and I sold them on Salahita for a good profit. We sailed on from there to the land of Sindh, where I saw many wonders, then westwards to Basrah, where I parted company with the ship and the travelers, and traveled back upriver to Baghdad.

Once home, I settled down again, distributing alms to the poor, helping widows and orphans, and living well, eating and drinking in comfort with my friends. But that was not my last voyage ... I will tell you more tomorrow, if you return.

And with that, Sinbad the Sailor turned once more to feasting. As the day ended, he once again sent his new friend home with another gift of a hundred dinars, and Sinbad the Porter resolved to hear the fourth tale.

The Fourth Voyage: Cannibals and Caves of Terror

The next morning, Sinbad the Porter rose, said the morning prayers, and hurried to the house of Sinbad the Sailor, where he was made welcome as before.

At length, when all his guests were present, Sinbad the Sailor spoke again. You have heard me tell, he began, that I had returned home from my third voyage to a life of comfort. But even as I ate and drank, my impetuous, dangerous spirit was stirring, reminding me of the wonders I had seen and the profits I had made, and making me forget past hardships.

And so, one day, I purchased a load of valuable goods, packed them in bales, and journeyed down to Basrah, where I gathered a party of merchants about me. We found a ship and set sail. For a while we did well, trading profitably from port to port.

But then the wind turned stiffly against us in mid-ocean. The captain ordered sea anchors to be dropped, but the storm turned ever more savage, throwing the vessel about on the waters. First the sails were ripped to shreds, and then the gale whipped up a vast wave which came crashing down upon us, smashing the ship to fragments.

I was thrown into the water with everyone else, and for what seemed like hours we struggled to keep afloat. At length, though, one of the ship's largest timbers came floating past. Some of us grasped hold of it, then clambered astride. No longer needing to swim for our lives, but driven by the wind, we came after a day or two to an island, where the sea cast us up on the shore.

We staggered to our feet and set out to explore. We found plants, some of them edible, so we were no longer in immediate danger of starvation, although we were still cold and desperate. Then, as we looked further from the shore, we saw before us a strange tower.

We approached cautiously, until suddenly a crowd of naked men erupted from the doorway, laid hands on us without a word, and drew us inside. There, we found a more imposing figure seated on a throne, evidently the king. He gestured for us to sit, and then he made a sign to his naked subjects. Some of them went off and returned with bowls of unfamiliar food.

All of my companions fell eagerly upon this meal, for we still were famished. But something about it turned my stomach, and I restrained myself. Thanks be to Allah for my self-restraint! For when they ate the food, my companions quickly became stupefied and dazed, and they began to eat voraciously. Then the naked men brought cups of oil, some of which they gave my companions to drink and some of which they used to anoint their heads. This had an even greater effect, for my companions' eyes rolled back in their heads and they ate ever more madly.

I became fearful for the others, and so I paid close attention to the men of that land. I soon realized to my horror that they were devil-worshippers, and that their king was actually a demonic *ghul*. Over the next few days, I learned something even worse. These naked men were cannibals, and they evidently treated all strangers who came to their land the same way, using the food and oil to reduce them to beasts. The victims' bellies would swell up, they would lose all power of thought, and then they would be given over to the care of a herdsman, who would take them out into the pastures around that building, where they would crawl around eating on all fours. Then, when they were fat,

Sinbad meets people from many exotic cultures on his travels. Here, he is shown discussing geography with Indian scholars. (© North Wind Picture Archives / Alamy)

they would be slaughtered. The *ghul*-king ate his man-flesh roasted, while his subjects liked theirs raw.

Fortunately, because I avoided this trap, eating only what little wholesome food I could scavenge, I not only retained my wits, but remained thin and bony. Because of this, the cannibals lost interest in me, for I would have made a poor meal. So it was that one day, I was able to slip away from the group and avoid the attention of any of the naked men.

As I made my way cross country, I saw a figure sitting on a rock, keeping watch. It was the herdsman. He saw me, but did not raise the alarm. Instead, he took pity on me, like a farmer taking pity on a worthless animal. He waved to me, and then indicated one of the paths leading away from that place, somehow conveying that it would lead to safety. Glad of the hope of escape, I followed his directions, soon breaking into a terrified run. At the end of the day, I collapsed exhausted, scavenging what edible herbs I could find. I could not sleep for fear of pursuing cannibals, but rose in the middle of the night and continued on my way.

And so I continued for seven days and seven nights, trudging ever onwards across the plains in the midst of the island and scavenging just enough food to avoid starvation. On the eighth day, though, I saw something ahead of me. For a moment I paused, fearing that I would find yet another danger, but I soon saw that this was a group of civilized-looking men, gathering peppercorns. I approached carefully and, when they saw me, they surrounded me, asking who I was and how I came there.

In reply, I told them that I was a shipwrecked traveler who had just come here from across the island. "But how did you escape the cannibals?" they asked. "That part of the land is full of those savages." And so I told them the rest of my story, and they congratulated me on my escape.

They gave me food and drink, and let me rest while they finished their work. Then we all embarked on a ship which had brought them to this island, and sailed to their home island not far away. There, they presented me to their king, who listened to my story with interest, and gave me food and drink. I looked around their city, finding it wealthy, prosperous, and orderly, while their king treated me as a guest.

One thing that I soon noticed, though, was that many of the people rode very fine horses, but none used saddles. And so of course I asked the king why this was.

"What is this *saddle*?" he asked in reply. "I have never heard of such a thing."

"It is something that makes riding much more comfortable, and allows better control of the horse," I said. "If you like, I can show you."

The king was interested, and he gave orders that I should be given what I needed for the purpose. And so I found a skilled carpenter, who made a frame to my orders. I used my own skills to pad this with wool and cover it with leather, which I polished until it shone. I attached a girth, and I then found a blacksmith to make a bit and stirrups. Then I had a horse brought from the king's stables, and saddled and harnessed it.

I brought the horse before the king. He mounted the saddle, and he was pleased at the comfort and control that it and the harness gave him. He smiled on me and gave me a generous reward.

During his fourth voyage, Sinbad is lowered into the Caves of the Dead – in slightly more comfort in this illustration than the story suggests.

When the king's vizier saw how useful the saddle was, he asked me to make him another like it. Soon, all the great men of the court wanted saddles, and I went into business with the carpenter and the blacksmith to supply them. Thus I made a fortune and continued to be honored in the court.

One day, as I sat conversing with the king, he turned to me and said, "Good Sinbad, you must know that I have come to love you like a brother. I cannot bear the thought that you might one day leave my city. Hence, I have a favor to ask you, which I must ask you not to refuse."

"I can refuse none of your commandments, great king," I replied. "What is your request?"

"There is among the court a certain lady," he said. "She is beautiful and intelligent, from a good and wealthy family, and she was brought up here, so she is cultured and refined. I would ask you to marry her. If you do this, I will provide the two of you with a goodly house close by the palace."

I was struck dumb with embarrassment at this honor, so the king looked on me with concern, and asked why I did not speak. "Great king," I stammered when I was able, "I can refuse none of your commands."

And so the lady was brought before us, and the king sent for a judge to marry us. He was as good as his word, providing not only a house but also servants and slaves. My new wife too was just as he described, and I soon came to love her dearly, and she me. I did still hope one day to return to Baghdad, but I decided that if that became possible somehow, I would happily take her with me.

However, none of us can know what destiny has in store. There came a day when I heard that the wife of one of my neighbors had died, and I hurried to his house to pay my respects. When I arrived, I found him weeping, and so I tried to console him. "Your loss is sad," I said to him, "but do not despair. Your own life goes on. Better times will come."

But my neighbor scowled at me. "How so?" he said. "How can better times come when I have but a day to live?"

"That is foolishness," I said. "Whatever your sadness, you are still healthy. You have years of life before you."

"No," he said, "you do not know the custom of this land. When a husband dies, or a wife, the one who is married to them is buried along with them. None may survive to enjoy life after their husband or wife has died!"

"By Allah!" I said, "That is an awful custom!"

But as we spoke, a group of citizens of the town arrived. They consoled my neighbor on the loss of his wife and on his own fate. They had brought a coffin, and they laid out his wife's body, properly dressed and with jewellery to make her look as fair as possible in death. Then they carried the coffin out of town, and we all made our way up the lower slopes of a great mountain that overlooked the sea.

We came to a great boulder, which members of the party rolled aside, revealing a deep cave. First, they lowered the coffin in, and then my neighbor, weeping but accepting his fate, stepped forward. They handed him seven loaves and a pitcher of water, and then they tied a rope around his waist and lowered him too into the cave. I could just see him when he reached the bottom of the pit, and he untied the rope from his waist. Then the other mourners pulled the rope up, rolled the boulder back to close the pit's mouth once more, and made their way sadly back to the city.

I was horrified, and when I was back home, I made my way to the king and asked how it was that his people should bury the living along with the dead.

"That is our custom, handed down from our ancestors," he said simply. "No husband and wife should be separated by death."

"O king," I said, "if the wife of a foreigner like myself should die in your land, would he too be buried along with her?"

"Indeed," said the king.

At this, I was struck to the heart with fear, lest my wife should die and I should be consigned to that miserable death. I told myself not to worry, for we might both live yet for many years, and I might well die before her, for no

Sinbad among the dead.
During his fourth voyage,
Sinbad finds himself trapped
alive in a great communal
tomb.

man knows the hour of his doom. And so I returned to my amusements and tried to distract myself.

And yet, my fate was to be all that I feared. It was not very long after learning of these traditions that my beloved wife fell ill, and although I paid for the best doctors and medicines, she soon succumbed to the sickness and died. And then the townsfolk and the king came to me, offering me and her family their sympathy. They brought a coffin, and she was laid out in her finest clothes and richest jewellery. And then they lifted the coffin and laid hands on me, and we traveled out to the mountain overlooking the sea, where the rock was rolled aside and my wife's coffin was lowered into the pit.

Then they turned to me. I cried out, protesting that I was a foreigner and not bound by their customs, but they did not listen, but held me still and tied me up, also binding a bag holding seven loaves and a pitcher of water to me. Then they lowered me into the place of coffins and bodies.

I worked free of their bindings, and they called to me to untie the rope that was around my waist, but I refused, defying them. So they hurled the rest of the rope down on top of me, rolled the boulder back over the pit's mouth, and left me there to die.

I looked around me. I could see little in the scant light that came through the gaps around the boulder, but I could see mounds of corpses and smell the stench of decay. I wept in the darkness, thinking that this was worse than the other deaths I had faced. But once again, I found myself determined to live, although I could not see any escape. I found a space to sleep that was free of bodies and bones and carefully refrained from drinking any of my water until I was parched or eating any of my bread until I was starving.

Then, just as my supplies were beginning to run out, there came a day when I heard movement overhead. I hid in a corner of the cave, watching as the boulder was moved aside and a coffin was lowered in, followed by a weeping woman with her bag of food.

It came to me that this was one of the people of the city that had condemned me to this horrible death, and that she was herself resigned to her doom and already as one dead, by these accursed customs. And so, I waited until the boulder had been replaced and my eyes were once more adapted to the darkness, and then I crept up behind her, clutching a human shin bone that I picked up from the cave floor.

The woman did not hear me, and I struck her on the head with the bone, and she fell unconscious. I struck twice again, and she ceased to breathe. I noticed that she was wearing much fine jewellery and gold necklaces, by way of grave goods, but that concerned me less than her food and drink, which I took to sustain me for several more days.

Within that period, another burial party came to the pit, and I slew the living man who was lowered into the tomb taking his food and water, too. And so I continued for some time, killing to live.

And then, one night, as I slept in my corner of the cave, I was awoken by the sound of movement. I leapt to my feet and picked up my shin bone club, but then I heard something scurrying away into a side cave. Carefully following, I saw a dim light ahead of me. Scarcely daring to hope, I approached and saw that there was a narrow tunnel. Hearing the scurrying still ahead of me, I realized what had happened. Scavenging animals had caught the smell of decay and had burrowed their way in. Suddenly, I had hope of escape! I fell on my knees and gave thanks.

And then I pushed myself into the tunnel, expanding it with my hands and shoulders as the light grew brighter ahead of me. Soon, I emerged into morning daylight and air free of the reek of death. Looking around, I saw that I was on a deserted beach. Once I was fully out of the tunnel, I explored a short way and realized that this small beach was cut off entirely from the rest of the island by the bulk of the mountain and could never be visited by men.

Once I had recovered my breath, I made my way back through the tunnel and gathered up my current supplies of bread and water. Then another thought came to me, and I also collected up the most valuable grave goods around the cave. I also found the best clothes that had been worn by those I had slain, to replace my own garments, which had been reduced to rags, and fashioned other clothes and funeral shrouds into bags in which to carry things.

And so I transported everything out to the open. Glad though I was to be free of the mass tomb, there was little to eat or drink on the beach, and so every day I made my way back into the cave, and every time there was another funeral, I renewed my supplies by slaying the living spouse.

But most of the time, I kept watch from the beach, until one day my prayers were answered, and I saw a ship sailing past. I snatched up a stick to which I had fastened a white shroud, and I ran along the beach, waving frantically. My luck held, and someone aboard the ship saw me, and they stopped, turned towards the island, and sent a boat ashore to collect me.

They asked how I had come to that beach, because the captain swore that, in all the years he had sailed this route, he had never seen any man there. I told them that I was a merchant who had been aboard a ship that was wrecked, but I had managed to load some of my luggage onto a broad beam from the wreck and had then been cast up on that shore. I did not mention the tomb, for fear that people from the city might be on the ship.

I also offered the captain gifts from among my goods, in gratitude for my rescue, but he refused, saying that it was his custom to rescue shipwrecked travelers without payment. At that, I called down the blessings of Allah upon him.

And so we sailed on, though, my sleep was full of nightmares of the cave and of how I had survived by killing, so that I thought I might go insane. At length, though, the ship came to Basrah, where I parted from the captain and his crew. Then I made my way to Baghdad, where I met my family and

(OVERLEAF)
Sinbad has just escaped after being buried alive in a cave-tomb, finding a tunnel out to an otherwise inaccessible beach. He has sighted a passing ship and attracted the crew's attention, and the crew have sent a boat to pick him up. Fortunately, perhaps, they do not recognize that the clothes he is wearing, and the bundles he is carrying, are actually burial shrouds – despite the fact that they are the white color typical of funerary garb from the region.

Sinbad is well into his 30s by now, but he has just had a terrifying, dangerous, and brutal experience, which has forced him to act as a ruthless killer, so he is looking gaunt and haunted. Once again, the depiction of the ship here is based on modern attempts to reconstruct a 9th-century Arab merchant dhow. One important feature is that it is assembled entirely without metal nails or bolts; the planks are literally sewn together and attached to the frame and keel with thick coconut fiber cords.

household, sold the valuable goods which I had scavenged from the dead, and returned to my old life.

I gave alms to the poor and lived in luxury, and time brought me relief from nightmares. My ability to forget the terrors of my travels saved my sanity, but once again it allowed my desire to travel the world to take control of me, so that even this was not my last voyage ... But that is tomorrow's tale.

Then Sinbad the Sailor had a fine meal set before his guests, and he gave another gift of one hundred dinars to Sinbad the Porter, who returned to his modest home, wondering at what he had heard.

The Fifth Voyage: Rocs, Again, and the Old Man of the Sea

The next day, Sinbad the Porter rose, said his morning prayers, and returned to the great house of Sinbad the Sailor, as had become his custom. Once they had saluted each other, and all the other guests were present, Sinbad the Sailor told his fifth tale.

Once again, he said, I forgot the terrors that I had suffered and became determined to travel. Once again, I acquired trade goods and sailed down to Basrah. There, at the docks, I saw a newly-built ship, strongly constructed with graceful lines. Being wealthy from my previous adventures, I decided on a whim to buy it for my own, and I appointed a captain and crew, to be supervised by my own clerks and servants. A number of merchants paid me

Sinbad learns a healthy respect for rocs when he first encounters one, but unfortunately, his companions during a second encounter are less wise. Here, Gustave Doré shows them breaking a roc's egg and killing its chick.

well to travel on this vessel, and we set sail.

We traveled for some time from land to land, making good profits, until one day we came to an uninhabited island. Many of the merchants and crew went ashore to rest and relax, but I remained aboard, to supervise and because I had suffered so many bad experiences on such islands.

After a while, one of the merchants who had been ashore came back, looking greatly amused. "Do come and see," he said, "we found what we took for a great white dome with no entrance. And so we struck it with rocks to test what it might be, and it began to shatter. I believe that it is naught but a giant egg!"

When I heard this, I was filled with dread, so I instantly went ashore and hurried where the merchant was pointing. I was too late, however. As I had guessed, the "dome" was the egg of a roc, and now it was shattered. A flood of liquid rushed out, then the chick within emerged. The others promptly killed it with their swords and thrown stones, and they began butchering it, roasting the meat on a fire and happily discussing the flavour.

"Stop, you fools," I cried out. "That was the egg of a roc, and where there are eggs, there are parents. What do you think that the roc will do when it sees its child slain?"

Sinbad's fifth voyage involves a second encounter with giant rocs. On this occasion, they destroy the ship which Sinbad bought for his own by bombarding it with huge boulders.

At first, the fools ignored me. But then something moved across the face of the sun, and, when we all looked up, we saw a roc, returning, just as I expected. Then they all panicked and leapt to their feet, and we rushed back to the ship.

As we climbed aboard, I ordered the captain to set sail immediately and run before the wind. But even as we left the island behind us, I looked back and saw not one but two rocs circling high above – both the parents. They saw us and screamed in rage.

Then, though, they turned away, and for a moment we had hope. But soon they returned, each of them carrying a gigantic boulder in its claws. The first of them dropped its boulder when directly above us, but the captain used all his skill and threw himself against the rudder even as the boulder fell, turning the ship aside just far enough.

Another depiction of the rocs sinking Sinbad's ship during his fifth voyage. (© North Wind Picture Archives / Alamy)

Our escape did not last for long, however. The waves from that first impact threw us around on the sea, and the chaos was almost enough to draw us under. Before the captain could regain control, the second roc dropped a smaller boulder. It struck my ship directly on the stern, shattering the rudder, killing the captain where he stood, and slamming what was left of the vessel down into the waters. We were all thrown into the sea, and the rocs departed, satisfied with their revenge.

Most of the crew and merchants drowned, but once again fortune and determination saved my life. I grasped hold of one of the larger timbers, clambered astride it, and began to paddle with my feet. At length, when I was almost dead from exhaustion, I came to another island, where the waves cast me up on the shore. I lay for a while, recovering my breath, and then rose and looked around.

Sinbad and the Old Man of the Sea as depicted by the famous illustrator H. J. Ford.

I was pleased to discover that the island, although it seemed deserted, was a veritable paradise, with fruit trees, sweet springs, and birdsong filling the air. When I had eaten of the fruit and drunk of the water, night was falling, and I lay down to sleep.

The next morning, I set out to explore further, and after a while I came upon a strange new sight. Seated on the bank of a stream was a venerable old man, clad in nothing but a kilt of leaves. I thought that he must be another shipwrecked traveler like myself, and so I greeted him. He said nothing in reply, however, and so I asked him who he was and how he had come there. Again he said nothing, but gestured, pointing to the stream, indicating that he wished to cross and suggesting that I carry him.

It seemed to me that this would be an act of charity which Allah might reward, and so I lifted him onto my shoulders and waded across the stream. When I reached the other side, I crouched down so he should get down. He did not do so, however, but wrapped his legs tightly around my neck.

Then I truly looked at those legs for the first time, and saw that they were covered in dark skin, tough as leather. I was unnerved, and I attempted to throw the old man off. But his legs were every bit as strong as they looked. He wrapped them even more tightly around my throat, throttling me until

WHO WAS THE OLD MAN?

For those who want to find some real-world basis for things that appear in Sinbad's tales, there are various possible explanations for the Old Man of the Sea. In the footnotes to his translation of *The Arabian Nights*, Sir Richard Burton offered a selection, including references to Greek myth. One of his suggestions that remains popular is that the image came from stories of the orangutan of Sumatra; the appearance of a wizened old man, the leathery skin on the legs, and the diet of fruit, all correspond quite well. The real orangutan is a rather cautious (though physically formidable) ape, but local superstitions do sometimes credit it with being dangerously intelligent and almost supernatural, and such stories may have been passed on to visiting seafarers.

However, Burton actually preferred another theory; some East African societies which kept slaves apparently did employ them for riding, much as in the story. Of course, more than one travelers' tale from around the Indian Ocean may have ended up mixed together.

I collapsed and nearly fell unconscious. Then, as I recovered, he beat and battered me with his feet until I staggered to my feet, and then he leaned forward and gestured that I should carry him to a nearby grove of fruit trees.

When we arrived there, he plucked the best and ripest fruit in reach, gobbling everything up greedily. Then he directed me to other trees, and so we went from place to place, with him eating the best food to be found on the island. From time to time, he would void his bladder or bowels down my back, and if ever I delayed or seemed to be defying him, he would beat me savagely with his legs.

This went on for many days. If the old man wished to sleep, he would doze briefly, but the grip of his legs would not slacken even then. He allowed me only snatched moments of sleep and food scavenged from what he left. I cursed my ill fortune and the pity that had made me try to help him.

Then, one day, I found a number of gourds lying around one part of the island, some of them dry and hollow. I had a small idea and, in one of my brief moments of rest, I picked up one of these, made an opening in it, and cleaned it out. Then, I found a grapevine, took some grapes, and squeezed their juice into the gourd. Then I stoppered it and left it in the sun.

Another depiction of Sinbad and Old Man of the Sea. Here, the Old Man is depicted as a curious merman-like creature, rather than the seemingly human figure described in the story. (Bridgeman Art Library)

I repeated this with more of the gourds in snatched moments and then, after a few days, I went back to the first. I found that, as I hoped, the juice had fermented, and become a sort of wine. I drank this and found it helped me endure my suffering.

After another little while, the old man saw me drinking from a gourd, and he gestured towards it questioningly. "It is something invigorating," I told him, for I was quite drunk at the time, and I went running and dancing through the trees, regardless of the weight on my shoulders. Then the old man snatched the gourd from my hands.

He drank deep, swallowing all the wine. This made him as drunk as you would expect, and he began to sway on my shoulders. To my delight, I felt his legs loosen and, as I sank carefully to the ground, he let go his grip and slumped on the forest floor, snoring.

Overjoyed to be free at last, I looked around until I found a good big stone. I picked this up in both hands, carried it over to my tormentor, and

ALCOHOL

Anyone who knows a little about traditional Muslim law may be startled to see wine appearing in Sinbad's tales. Sinbad drinks to help him endure the situation with the Old Man of the Sea, but there are also hints of wine-drinking at parties.

In fact, *The Arabian Nights* takes a relaxed view of the Muslim prohibition on alcohol. Many stories feature characters drinking wine, and this does not automatically make them into villains. The fact is that, despite the Koran's fairly clear prohibition of alcohol, historically many Muslims finessed the rules or just ignored them. Only the most puritanical Islamic states had total legal prohibition, and some poets and mystics even praised wine. In *The Arabian Nights*, the Caliph Haroun al-Rashid is frequently shown as a social drinker, although the real man may have been more austere.

Also, readers might think that grape juice would probably not ferment into even the roughest of drinkable wine after only a few days. However, in the world where these stories originated, people may have been more familiar with a kind of very low-strength "wine" made by soaking raisins or dried dates in water and letting the liquid ferment for a day or two, or with the "toddy" made from palm tree sap in Asia and Africa, which ferments to modest strength within a day. Hence Sinbad's story would not have sounded particularly outrageous.

brought it down on the old demon's head with all my strength. With one blow, I smashed his skull and killed him. May Allah have no mercy on him!

Then I went down to the beach, cleaned myself in the sea, and began gathering fruit and water. I lived thus for a few days, until one day a ship came past and dropped anchor, and some of the crew came ashore to gather supplies. I hurried up to them, and they were startled to see me, so I told them my story.

"Allah be praised!" they said. "Stories tell of that fiend who enslaved you. He was called the Old Man of the Sea. But no one has ever escaped him before!"

And so they took me aboard, and we sailed away. At length, the ship came to a great city which they said was called the City of the Apes. I went ashore to look around, not knowing that the ship was set to leave soon, and they must have thought that I had found somewhere I wished to be, for they sailed without me.

As I wandered around the docks, some local people came up to me, seeing that I was a stranger. I explained my situation, and they told me to come aboard a boat at once. Looking around, I saw that everyone in the city seemed to be doing the same, and so I joined them. We put out to sea a little way as the sun set, and then, watching the darkened city, I saw scurrying movement and heard screeching and howling.

The local folk explained to me why their city had its name. "Every night, countless apes come into the city," they explained. "By day, they live in the forests and mountains, but we cannot stop them using our buildings at night. They are strong and savage, and they kill any man they find still ashore."

And so we rested on the waves, and then returned ashore after the sun rose. As we rowed into the docks, my new companions asked if I had a trade which could earn me a living.

(OPPOSITE)

A weird, seemingly human figure, the Old Man of the Sea, has tricked Sinbad into carrying him on his shoulders, then locked his muscular legs around Sinbad's neck, and is using Sinbad as a slave. Here, Sinbad has hit on a way to escape, manufacturing rough wine in gourds which he has found around the forest. Sinbad himself is already happily drunk; when the Old Man, who has never encountered wine before, drinks himself into a stupor, he will release his grip.

Sinbad's improvised bottle, as seen in this picture, may be a green calabash or a bottle gourd, which is used as a container in many places around the Indian Ocean.

Another depiction of Sinbad and the Old Man of the Sea, here in a more fairy-tale style. (Mary Evans Picture Library)

"No," I said. "I am a merchant. But my ship was wrecked and my stock was lost."

"In that case," one of them said, "I can assist you, if fortune favors you. Here, take this bag, go down to the seashore, and gather up as many pebbles as you can carry. A group of men will be along later to do the same; they are friends of mine, and I will tell them to help you."

I was puzzled, but I had no other ideas, and so I obeyed, collecting pebbles in the bag, then going along with the party from the city when they appeared. They led me to a forested valley and, looking up, I saw apes in the treetops, staring down at us. These creatures were not so bold in daylight! My companions stopped, reached into their bags, and produced their stones, which they used to pelt the apes. I followed their example. The apes responded with fury, screeching and howling, and began to retaliate.

Dodging their missiles, I looked closer and realized that they were in fact coconuts. The apes could be provoked to pick this fruit for us! After a few minutes, we all gathered up as many coconuts as we could carry and hurried back to the city well before nightfall. I returned to my new friend from the night before and offered him the coconuts which I had collected, but he told me to keep them and trade them.

So that is how I lived for a while, spending my nights on the water and my days collecting coconuts. By hard work and careful trading, I turned a decent profit, and I was soon able to recompense my local friends for their assistance.

Then, one day, a merchant ship came into port, which I learned was bound for Basrah. And so I went to my new friends, thanked them for their aid, and said my farewells. Then I took my accumulated stock of best-quality coconuts and some money which I had saved, went to the ship's captain, and paid him for passage.

We sailed from island to island and, starting with my stock of coconuts, I traded for local goods, for peppers, cinnamon, and agarwood. When we came to an island of pearl-fishers, I hired local divers and, by good fortune added fine pearls to my stock too.

And so it was that by the time I came to Basrah and thence to Baghdad, I had more than restored the fortune with which I had set out. Back home, I gave gifts to my family and alms to the poor, and I settled down again – until such time as my wanderlust overcame me again. For you must know by now that I was forever making the same error. Tomorrow, I will tell you of my sixth voyage.

And so, Sinbad the Porter returned to his home that night with his accustomed gift, wondering what he would hear of his new friend's sixth adventure.

The Sixth Voyage: The River of Gems

The next day, Sinbad the Porter returned to the fine mansion, exchanged greetings, ate and drank with the other guests as before, and listened.

I had settled down in peace after my fifth voyage, said Sinbad the Sailor, and I thought that I might now remain in Baghdad. But one day, a party of

Shipwreck is a hazard frequently faced by Sinbad and those with whom he travels – as illustrated here. (North Wind Picture Archives)

Sinbad improvises a raft for travel on an underground river during his sixth voyage. This depiction shows an impressively substantial construction. (Mary Evans Picture Library)

merchant venturers came to visit me, and again I remembered the fascination of travel. Even with all that I had suffered, I could think of no greater joy than returning to my home and seeing my friends again after long parting.

And so, yet again, I acquired a stock-in-trade and traveled down to Basrah. There, I took passage with a sizeable company of prosperous merchants, and we voyaged and traded successfully for some time.

But one day, as we were sailing upon seas whipped up by a stiff breeze, the captain, who had been taking sightings, set up an unhappy wailing. We merchants looked to see him rending his garments, plucking at his beard, beating his brow, and then throwing himself down on the deck.

"What is the matter?" we asked.

"We are lost!" the captain cried. "The wind has carried us into a sea wherein I know not the routes or currents, and even now it drives us to our doom!"

And indeed, when we looked through the sea spray, we saw that we were being carried towards a great island which, in the nearest part, rose steeply from the water like a mountain. The captain called commands to his crew, clambered up the mast himself, and attempted to lower the sail. But the wind was too strong and snatched the rigging from his hands. A great gust threw the ship about, smashing the rudder as the crew struggled with it. All control lost, we cried out farewells to each other as we were hurled directly into the island.

In a moment, the ship was reduced to driftwood. Many of my companions were drowned, but some of us managed to swim ashore and drag ourselves clear of the waves. We looked and saw that ours was not the first ship to be wrecked here; the remains of many other vessels and their cargoes were scattered all about us.

Some of my companions wandered dazed through this wreckage, but I kept my wits enough to climb a promontory and look around. This stretch of shore was cut off from the rest of the island by high mountains, and it seemed largely barren. There were a few streams, the greatest of which poured out of a gorge in the rocks and into a sinkhole nearby, and little vegetation save for a few trees. Some of them were the sorts that provide agarwood, but none gave edible fruit. I also found to my amazement a spring that produced ambergris instead of water. This was liquid enough in the heat of the day that it flowed down to the sea, and in the next few days I saw great sea monsters, attracted by its scent, swim up to the coast and devour it. I am told that it is transformed in their bellies, and that they eventually vomit it up, and it then congeals on the surface of the water into the form that perfume makers know. In that place, though, when the pure stuff melted in the daytime sun, the air was filled with its musky scent. When I came to the largest stream, I discovered the greatest wealth of all, for its bed and banks were studded with precious stones – rubies and emeralds, and sapphires, in such profusion that the very ground glittered in the sun!

So we who had survived the wreck were stranded among a fortune, and yet we were doomed to die by starvation. We gathered up what food we had and rationed it out carefully, a bare mouthful a day, and so we soon grew

THE ORIGINS OF AMBERGRIS

Of all the treasures that Sinbad acquires and trades, ambergris may seem the strangest. In reality, its origin isn't quite as described in his tale. It is a waxy solid that is used in perfume making as a fixative, enabling scents to last longer; it is very valuable, although in modern times it has mostly been replaced by synthetic fixatives.

It is in fact produced naturally in the intestines of sperm whales, possibly to ease the passage of sharp or hard objects that the whale has swallowed. It is then usually excreted with faeces, but, may sometimes be vomited up. "Fresh" ambergris thus smells unpleasant, but as it floats on the sea, it hardens and develops its distinctive musky smell. Lumps are collected for sale when they wash up on beaches.

very hungry. No ships passed, and one by one my companions succumbed to starvation, exposure, or sickness caused by their sufferings. As they died, we did what we could to give them proper funerals, washing their bodies, wrapping them in winding-sheets made of fabrics recovered from the wrecks, and digging them graves where the ground allowed. At length, I alone was left, after burying my last companion.

When that was done, I cursed my folly for having yet again risked my life on the ocean when I could have stayed at home in comfort. Now I would die, without even a friend to wash my body and give me decent burial. I dug a grave by the shore and decided that, when I felt death approaching, I would lie in that and hope that, in time, at least the wind would cover me decently.

But then I found myself contemplating the stream which poured into that cavernous sinkhole at the base of the mountain. "By Allah," I thought, "that must go somewhere, and it cannot be anywhere worse than this. It might even carry me to safety. At worst, I will perish, but that is no worse than what will happen to me here."

And so I gathered up the stoutest branches I could find from the agarwood trees and lashed them together to form a raft, which I carefully made a little narrower than the mouth of the cave. Then I took planks from some of the wrecks and lashed them atop the branches to form a deck. Finally, I fixed stout, flat planks on either side of the raft to act as steering oars.

Then, not knowing what I might need if I survived, I found some sacks and gathered up precious stones, ambergris, and what little food I had left, loaded it onto my raft, then pushed it onto the stream and clambered aboard as the current took it. Hunching down low, I rode the stream to the mouth of the cavern and hurtled into darkness.

The stream carried me deep under the mountain, and soon the raft was bumping against the walls of the cave, first on one side and then on the other, while I had to lie flat to pass under the ceiling. I realized that if the cave grew much narrower the raft would be able to go no further, and I knew that I could not go back, and so I wondered if I had condemned myself to die in darkness. But my luck held, and the cave never quite became too narrow.

I know not how long I rode, flat on my face, jolting and bumping through darkness. At length, exhaustion overcame my terror, and I fell asleep, or perhaps just unconscious.

When I awoke, I was stunned to find myself not only in daylight, but surrounded by people. The raft had drifted to a riverbank, and these folk had caught it and tied it fast, and were now gathered around me. At first I thought that this must be a dream, and I did not know what to say, and they knew not what to make of me.

They had dark skins, like Indians or Ethiopians, and they were talking in a language which I did not recognize. After a while, though, one of them – perhaps a religious scholar or one who had dealt with merchants – spoke to me in Arabic.

Sinbad (John Phillip Law) fighting a stop-motion centaur in *The Golden Voyage of Sinbad* (1973). (© United Archives GmbH / Alamy)

"Peace be upon you, friend," he said. "How came you here? We never see boats on this stream!"

"I will tell you," I said, "but for the love of Allah, I beg you to give me some food, for I am starving."

At that, the man sent for food, and soon I was restored enough to tell my tale, as he translated to the others, who he told me were peasants who farmed the land around the stream. When I was done, they spoke among themselves, and then the Arabic speaker turned back to me. "This is a strange and marvellous story," he said. "Let us take you to our king. He will want to know of you."

And so, they led me to their city, carrying my raft and all that had been upon it behind me. Their king greeted me courteously, listened to my story, and congratulated me on my escape from death. Then I laid before him gemstones and agarwood and ambergris, and he offered me lodging in his palace while I recovered my strength.

I found that this was the great and wealthy island of Serendib, and the people of its capital treated me with courtesy. In return, I told them of my travels and of my homeland. The king was especially interested to learn of the Caliph Haroun al-Rashid, and of the caliph's piety and justice.

"He is indeed an admirable ruler," the king said when I was finished. "I think that I should send him a gift, as a sign of friendship, one ruler to another. I would ask you to bear it to him."

"To hear is to obey," I said. But I had no way to return to Baghdad at that time. A little later, however, I heard that some local people were preparing an ocean-going ship for a trading venture, and so I arranged to take passage with them.

The king sent the caliph a cup carved from a single ruby and embellished with pearls, a magical bed covered with the skin of a giant serpent, which protects anyone who sleeps on it from all diseases, and a beautiful slave girl, along with a great load of agarwood. He also gave me rich gifts.

The ship carried me westwards until at length we reached Basrah, where I disembarked and took passage upriver. When I reached Baghdad, I went at once to the palace and presented the gifts there, and then I returned to my own home. Soon, however, a messenger came, requiring that I attend upon the caliph. Haroun asked me about the gifts which I had delivered, and I told him my story. He was impressed, and ordered that this all be written upon a parchment in letters of gold, and placed in the archives.

And so I returned once more to my life of comfort. But that was not my final voyage. I will tell of that tomorrow.

And then, Sinbad the Sailor gave Sinbad the Porter his customary gift of gold, and the porter returned to his own home.

The Seventh Voyage: The Land of Winged Men

And so there came the day when Sinbad the Porter went to the house of Sinbad the Sailor to hear of the last voyage. After they had greeted each other and the audience had arrived, Sinbad the Sailor spoke.

I had thought that facing death upon a barren shore and only escaping doom by plunging into the bowels of the earth had cured me of wanderlust. But after some time at home, the urge to travel came upon me again. And so, as before, I traveled down to Basrah with trade goods and took ship.

My new companions were good company, and we sailed across the great ocean, buying and selling profitably until we reached the distant City of China. Then we set sail for home once more. But, out on the open sea, a headwind blew up and rapidly turned into a gale, driving us back along our path. As we struggled to protect our cargo from driving rain, the captain tucked his clothes into his belt and scrambled up the mast, looking around for land. Soon, though, he began to wail and pluck at his beard.

"What is the matter?" we asked.

"Pray for salvation!" he replied. "This accursed wind has driven us into the furthest ocean of the world!"

Then he descended and opened a chest which he kept on deck. He extracted books and charts, and bags of magical powders which enabled

The winged men in their non-human form as depicted by ªRu-Mor

him to determine the ship's position when all else failed. But when he had performed these procedures, he became more mournful still.

"We have been driven toward the shores of the Land of Kings," he explained. "Here lies the tomb of the great King Solomon himself! But no mortal man may venture here and hope to live. The sea is full of gigantic serpents and monstrous whales large enough to swallow ships whole!"

No sooner had he said this than the ship was lifted by a huge wave, and when it crashed down, we saw a whale, every bit as terrible as the captain had said, swimming towards us. Then, a moment later, a second, even larger whale appeared and swam towards the first. And just as we were saying our sad farewells to each other, a third whale, even larger than the first two, broke the surface nearby.

The three monsters began swimming around our ship, stirring up the waters as they decided whether to attack us or each other first. In that moment, my urge to live overcame my terror, and I rushed to the side of the ship, casting off all my clothes except my under-shirt so that they would not weigh me down in the water. At that very moment, the third whale lunged at the ship, its jaws open wide, while a great gust of wind slammed into the vessel, so that it shattered as the monster bit at it. I leapt into the sea as everyone else was cast aside or swallowed.

And then, the three monsters turned away, and suddenly I was alone on the stormy waters amidst a few planks. I grasped at one and held onto it with all my strength.

As I floated on the ocean, I cursed myself for a fool. "My sufferings are sent by Allah to punish my greed," I thought. "I have plentiful wealth and no need to risk my life for more!"

And so I made a solemn vow to Allah that, if somehow I survived, I would sail the seas no more. And then, after two days and nights, I was at last cast up on an island. I saw no inhabitants, but there were fruit trees and fresh springs, so I was able to restore myself, and soon I found a stream flowing rapidly across the landscape.

Remembering my previous adventure, I decided to make another raft. I lashed together branches from the unfamiliar trees with cords made from creepers. Then, with a prayer, I loaded the raft with fruit, launched it on the stream, and scrambled aboard.

For three days and nights, the stream carried me across the island; then I saw ahead a cave mouth at the base of a great mountain. Remembering the terrors of the underground river on Serendib, I tried to steer for the banks, but the stream swept me into the darkness. I was sure that I was going to die, but after a short time I emerged once more into daylight.

Now, the stream ran down a deep valley, and the waters became ever more turbulent. Just as I thought that I was sure to drown in the rapids, I came to a city. People on the banks saw me and threw nets and ropes out to me. I grasped these, and they pulled me to safety.

I staggered off the raft, delirious with fear and lack of sleep, and people crowded around me, babbling questions which I could not answer. A venerable old man approached me and wrapped me in fine clothes. He escorted me to the public baths, then took me home and gave me food. I spent the next three days in his house, being tended by his servants, while I recovered myself enough to tell him my history. He proved kind, and a good Muslim, though many of the customs of that land seemed strange to me.

On that fourth day, he came to me and asked, "Would you like to come with me down to the riverbank and sell your goods? That should earn you enough to start trading."

I was struck dumb, not knowing what he was talking about, but he smiled at my silence, and said, "Have no fear, my son, for I will ensure that you get a fair price. If no one makes an offer that you like, you can store your goods in my warehouse for a while."

I decided that I had best go with him, to find out what he meant. We walked down to the river, where I found a small crowd gathered round an auctioneer and something on the ground. To my astonishment, I saw that it was my raft.

The auctioneer saw my host and spoke to the crowd. "What am I bid for this load of finest sandalwood?" he asked. The bidding started at 100 dinars, and rapidly rose to 1,000.

Then my host turned to me. "Is that sufficient for you, or should I store the sandalwood?" he asked. "You know better than I what is fair," I replied.

My host turned to the auctioneer. "One thousand and one hundred dinars," he called. That was the highest bid, and so my host summoned his servants to carry the sandalwood to his warehouse. Then he took me home and gave me the money.

I stayed with him a while longer as I learned the ways of trade in the city. I discovered that he was one of its leading merchants, and he treated me with great affection. Then one day he came to me. "I have a proposal for you," he said.

"Whatever I can do to repay your generosity, I will do," I replied.

"I am an old man," he said, "a widower with no sons. But I do have a beautiful daughter, who will inherit my fortune on my death. Would you marry her and take over my business? I feel that you would make a fitting heir."

Once again, I was struck dumb by his generosity, but when I recovered myself, I told him that I would obey his wishes. And so he summoned a notary, and I was married to his daughter that day. She proved beautiful indeed, and I became the old merchant's business partner. A little later, he died a peaceful death, and I took his place.

As I learned more about the city, I discovered that the native men had a very strange secret. Once every month, their whole appearance changed, and they grew wings and flew off into the upper air, leaving their women and children behind. I thought this marvellous and curious, and so on that day when the men's appearances began to change, I approached one of them with whom I had become friendly and begged him to carry me with him. At first he was unwilling, but I pressed him for the favor, and eventually he assented. I did not tell anyone in my household, for fear of worrying them, but went with the man, holding firmly to his body as he grasped my clothes, grew wings, and took flight. We rose higher and higher until we approached the very vault of heaven, where I heard the angels themselves singing. "Glory and praise be to Allah!" I cried out.

At that very moment, a burst of fire erupted from heaven above, almost consuming all of us. With a scream of rage, the winged men plummeted downwards. The one who was carrying me swooped down to a high mountaintop, cast me off with a dark curse, and flew away.

Alone in this high wilderness, I despaired of finding a way home and cursed my own folly in yet again seeking out adventures. After a few moments, however, I saw two figures approaching, young men of uncanny comeliness, each carrying a staff of red gold. I approached and saluted them, and they replied courteously.

"Who are you?" I asked.

"We are servants of Almighty Allah," they replied, and then one of them handed me another golden staff and indicated a path along a mountain ridge, saying that it led downwards. Then they walked away, and quickly vanished from sight.

I set out that way, wondering who they were, when suddenly a great serpent reared up from beside the ridge, and I saw that it was devouring a man, whom it had swallowed up to his navel. "Help me!" he cried "Whoever saves me, Allah shall save him!"

I stepped forward and struck the serpent on the head with my staff, at which it hissed, spat the man out, and slithered away. The man stood up and thanked me, saying that he would be my companion on the mountain. But then I saw a group of men approaching, and when I looked around, I could not see the man whom I had just saved. The group proved to be the men of the city, among them my supposed friend.

"Why did you abandon me?" I asked as politely as I could. "That was unworthy."

"You almost killed all of us," he replied. "You mentioned the name of Him who you worship. It is not safe to do so among us."

I apologized, saying that I did not know this, and promised not to repeat my error. And so, grudgingly, he grasped me and picked me up again.

My wife was overjoyed to see me, for I had been gone for some time. I told her of my adventure, and she sighed.

"You have now seen the true nature of these people," she said. "I did not think that you would believe me if I told you myself."

"What do you mean?" I asked.

"They are brothers to devils," she said. "They cannot even speak the name of Allah. It is unsafe for a Muslim to associate with them."

"But your father was a good Muslim, and so are you," I said.

"My parents were foreigners in this land," she explained. "They settled here, but they never followed the ways of this city. Even so, it is not a good place to be. My advice would be to depart this land."

I saw the wisdom of these words and decided to return to Baghdad. We sold all we could of my business and property, then found a ship in the harbor that was sailing westwards, took passage, and went aboard with all that we could carry. After a voyage of many days and nights, we reached Basrah, and I took passage upriver for the last time.

In the City of Peace, I placed my goods in storage and returned to my family home, where I greeted my kinsmen and introduced them to my wife. And then I gave thanks that my destiny was to come home safely once again, and settled down, truly resolved to keep my vow to travel no more.

And then, Sinbad the Sailor was done telling tales. Sinbad the Porter again asked forgiveness for the words he had spoken seven days before, but Sinbad the Sailor told him that he was already forgiven and gave him a last gift of a hundred dinars.

But even after that, Sinbad the Porter and Sinbad the Sailor became good friends. They met frequently in good fellowship, for neither wished ever to leave the City of Peace, save in stories. And so that was where both remained, all the days of their lives.

An Alternative Seventh Voyage

There is more than one early manuscript version of the Sinbad stories, and in some of these, the story of Sinbad's last voyage is significantly different. In fact, this version of the cycle (as found, for example, in Sir Richard Burton's translation of *The Arabian Nights*), is where the island which Sinbad visits on his *sixth* voyage is specifically identified as "Serendib" (or "Sarandib"), an old name for what is today called Sri Lanka (previously Ceylon); in other versions, Sinbad never finds out its name. Likewise, this version is the source of the list of specific gifts which the king of Serendib sends to Haroun al-Rashid. This is significant because of what follows.

After returning from that voyage, Sinbad firmly resolves to give up traveling, but Haroun, after receiving those gifts, decides to send a letter and gifts of his own in return, and he orders Sinbad to take them. Sinbad protests that he has sworn never to go to sea again; Haroun sympathizes, but Sinbad is the best person for the job, and a caliph's orders are not to be ignored.

So Sinbad sails to Serendib, delivers the gifts (including, according to various translations, a superb horse with a bejewelled saddle, silken garments, an agate vase, and furnishings including a table which belonged to King Solomon), and sets sail homewards. However, on the way, he is captured by pirates and sold into slavery.

His master gives him the task of killing elephants for their ivory, by hiding in a tree with a bow and arrows. This works well for a couple of months, but then the elephants evidently realize what is going on and identify the tree in which Sinbad is hiding, and one of them uproots it. Fortunately, though, instead of killing Sinbad, it picks him up and takes him deep into the forest, to a hill covered in the bones of elephants that had gone there to die (an example of the legendary "elephants' graveyard"). This of course can provide a vast supply of ivory; apparently, the elephants understand that this will save them from being hunted.

As the previous method was in fact (unknown to Sinbad) costing the lives of numerous slaves every year, Sinbad's master frees him in gratitude for his good fortune and sends him home with a gift of valuable ivory. Sinbad travels back to Baghdad by way of India and reports to the caliph.

The elephants' graveyard. The alternative version of Sinbad's seventh voyage involves a vast stroke of luck and some very forgiving elephants.

THE ARABIAN NIGHTS WORLD

Like most legends, the Sinbad stories say at least as much about the time and place in which they were told as about the places they describe. However, there was genuine continuity between the two; culturally, those stories may be a product of the later medieval Islamic world, but that world remembered earlier ages, spoke the same language, followed the same religion, and looked back to those earlier times with nostalgia and respect.

The Arabian Nights and the Sinbad cycle may have originated in Persia or even India, but the tales took something like their modern form in the coffeehouses and bazaars of the Arab world. *The Arabian Nights* probably arrived through Iraq in the 8th–10th centuries; the oldest surviving versions (without the Sinbad stories) come from medieval Syria, but the city most often associated with the telling of these tales is perhaps Cairo, in Egypt. Copies of the collection were circulating there by the 11th or 12th century, and European scholars acquired Arabic manuscripts and print editions there in the 18th and 19th centuries. So these are medieval stories seen through an Ottoman-period filter and probably influenced by European attempts to pin down shifting, unstable sources.

Haroun al-Rashid and the Abbasid Period

The stories in *The Arabian Nights* are set in many times and places, often just in a vague fantasy realm, but many of them, including the Sinbad stories, are supposedly set in the time of the Abbasid Caliph Haroun al-Rashid. The reason for this tradition is that Haroun's reign (786–809 AD) was seen as a time of greatness, when wonderful things were happening in the Muslim world, particularly among the Arabs.

The Caliphate

To start with, the Abbasid dynasty claimed the title of *caliph*. This means more than "emperor;" a caliph claims to be the "Successor to the Prophet Mohammed," a religious as well as a secular leader. It is generally implied that the caliph should have authority over most or all of the Muslim world, although this wasn't always the case in practice, especially when there were multiple claimants.

The Caliph Haroun al-Rashid, legendary ruler of Baghdad and most of the rest of the Muslim world in Sinbad's supposed time. Haroun is mentioned in the story of Sinbad's sixth voyage, and he makes a brief appearance in the alternative version of his seventh. (Bridgeman Art Library)

After Mohammed died in 632 CE, there was disagreement over who should lead his followers, with the title of caliph being created for this leader. Although there was always dispute about the rules for selecting the caliph, most early claimants were related to the prophet by blood in some way. After four caliphs selected from among Mohammed's close followers and family, the title fell to the Umayyad family, distant cousins of the prophet, who ruled for nearly a century until deposed (at least in the Middle East) by the Abbasids in 750 AD.

The Abbasid Rise and Haroun

The Abbasid family, descendants of one of Mohammed's uncles, built an efficient administration, a luxurious court, and the city of Baghdad. However, they were unable to control the vast conquests accumulated in the early years of Islamic expansion, so they handed whole provinces off to semi-independent governors, even permitting some distant provinces to break away entirely.

Haroun was one of the greatest Abbasids, and Arabs have long tended to mythologize him. He fought successful wars against the Byzantines, forged an alliance with China, and may have exchanged ambassadors with Europe's Charlemagne. His vizier for much of his reign was Yahya, a member of the Persian family of Barmakids; Yahya's son Ja'far seems to have been Haroun's personal friend. However, in 803 Haroun fell out spectacularly with the Barmakids, and had Ja'far executed and the rest of the family arrested. Ja'far too appears in some tales from *The Arabian Nights*, usually as Haroun's loyal right-hand man, though modern Hollywood "Arabian fantasy" movies usually seem to feature a duplicitous vizier or evil wizard named "Jafar."

Decline

After Haroun, Abbasid power went into decline; there were revolts during his reign and a war between his sons after his death. By the 11th century, the Abbasids were unable to stop the Seljuq Turks from taking over the Abbasid heartlands in Iraq, although the dynasty later managed something of a comeback and survived in Baghdad until 1258. In that year, the Abbasid Caliph al-Musta'sim was killed by the Mongols and the "Islamic Golden Age" came to an end.

Later rulers also claimed the title of caliph; the last major claimants were the Ottoman Turks, who lasted until the beginning of the 20th century. But the Abbasids were widely respected in retrospect, and Haroun became an important historical figure.

Medieval Baghdad

Haroun's capital, Baghdad, was founded on the Tigris River in 762 CE as the Abbasid capital, moving the center of power away from the previous capital of Damascus and closer to the homelands of their Persian civil service (Baghdad is just 19 miles, or 30 kilometers, from the old Persian capital of Ctesiphon). The city had access to good water supplies as well as trade routes, and it was carefully planned by the Caliph Mansur, grandfather of Haroun.

The core of the city was designed on a circular plan about a mile (1.6 km) in diameter, enclosing parks and gardens as well as residential, government, and commercial buildings, with the city mosque at the center. However, the bazaars were deliberately placed outside the walls of the Round City; Mansur didn't want spies or assassins sneaking in among crowds of shoppers.

Haroun also made the city a center of learning. Baghdad became a fabulously wealthy and impressive city during his reign, known officially as "the City of Peace" or "the Abode of Peace," and poetically as "the Bride of the World."

Basrah

Basrah is essentially the primary seaport for Iraq (although it doesn't have deep enough water for large modern ships), and hence for Baghdad. Founded in the early days of Islamic power, it lies 280 miles (450 km) as the crow flies downriver from the capital, where the Tigris and the Euphrates join to form the Shatt al-Arab waterway, which then flows down to the sea. Like Baghdad, it gained a reputation as an intellectual center under the Abbasids, but most of all, it has always been a port.

Seafarers on the Indian Ocean

Sailors had been operating in the Indian Ocean region since long before recorded history. The ancient Egyptians sent fleets down the Red Sea, and there is evidence of sea trade between Bronze Age Mesopotamia and the Indus Valley. Early sailors would have hugged the coasts, but it is thought that Greek sailors in the Hellenistic period worked out how to use the summer monsoon winds to sail directly from Arabia and the Horn of Africa to India, returning with the winter monsoon. By the time of the Roman Empire, traders were traveling from Roman-controlled territory to Ceylon, the Ganges Delta, the Malay Peninsula, and even China.

Political instability sometimes disrupted such trade, but the rise of Islam at the western end of the trade routes and the T'ang dynasty in China brought centuries of stability, and Persian and then Arab sailors not only reached China, but settled there. There was, apparently, a healthy Muslim community near the city of Guangzhou (Canton) by the 8th century, though unfortunately its members were not above dubious behavior, looting warehouses during a period of political chaos in 758 CE and being banned from the city for some years as a result. But they were allowed back in eventually, and Guangzhou was known in Arabia as an important if distant trade city. Sinbad's seventh tale, in which he visits the "City of China," is blown to the "furthest ocean of the world," and ends up in a remote city whose citizens follow strange and uncanny customs, but which still has Muslim residents, recalls this era of difficult but enduring trade between Iraq and coastal China.

But China was a long way away, and many of the stops on the way – India, Sri Lanka, Malaya – offered profits in their own right. Equally, Arab traders ventured down the east coast of Africa as far as Madagascar. The China trade probably went into decline after 878 CE, when Chinese rebels massacred the foreign merchant community in Guangzhou; both the T'ang dynasty and the Abbasids were fading by then. Still, Indian Ocean trade continued for centuries. However, it was never entirely safe; even in the early 20th century, it is said, one in ten voyages across the Indian Ocean did not reach its destination. And Sinbad's stories reflect more than relatively routine journeys from Arabia to India; they look like fantasy versions of expeditions to Sumatra or China, one-off ventures to make a captain's reputation and a merchant's fortune.

In any case, by the 14th century, the Chinese end of the route seems to have been controlled by Chinese ships. Then, in 1498, the Portuguese navigator Vasco da Gama arrived in East Africa and hired an Arab navigator to get him to India. From then on, big, sophisticated new European ships arrived in the region in ever-growing numbers and long-range Arab navigation went into long-term decline.

But it never entirely vanished, even if Arab sailors largely reverted to being coast-hugging local traders. Trade fleets were sailing out of Arabia more or less in living memory, and Arab *dhows* still operate in the region, although motors largely replaced sails in the second half of the 20th century.

Ships and Sailors

The *dhow* is certainly the type of ship traditionally associated with Arab sailing and the Sinbad stories. Despite the widespread introduction of engines, it is usually defined as a wooden sailing vessel with one or two masts; the size can vary a fair amount, and there is a large range of subtypes.

Although it is thought of as an Arab vessel, the *dhow* may have partly evolved in India, and a lot of Arab *dhows* were certainly built there, or constructed of Indian wood, usually teak or coconut; Arabia is notoriously short of trees. Wood used in shipbuilding in Oman could come from the Malabar Coast, nearly 1,300 miles (2,092 km) away. Coconut trees were also important because these ships were built without nails; the planks were sewn together with coconut-fiber cords. Iron nails only came into use in the 15th century. Sewn ships may not be as robust in general, but they may have been more flexible and able to withstand being run ashore, and they were almost certainly significantly cheaper to build.

Dhows are generally assumed to have triangular lateen sails, especially these days, and the Arabs have traditionally been credited with inventing that type of rigging, but some modern scholars now dispute this, suggesting that lateen sails originated in the Mediterranean. Whatever the details, though, the lateen

IBN BATTUTA

The medieval Islamic world extended from Spain to Sumatra and East Africa, and while it was not always at peace, it was culturally fairly unified. Hence, travelers could seriously contemplate traveling from one end of it to the other, and stories such as those of Sinbad, of journeys to lands far beyond the horizon, would not have sounded totally incredible.

The greatest real-life traveler of that world – perhaps the nearest thing to a real-life Sinbad – was Ibn Battuta, a native of Morocco. Unlike Sinbad, Ibn Battuta traveled by land as well as sea, often with a retinue of servants and even a harem, but he too suffered shipwrecks and pirates.

He was born in 1304 into a family of legal scholars, and at the age of 21 he set out on the traditional Muslim pilgrimage to Mecca, by way of Egypt. Somewhere along the way he developed an overwhelming wanderlust, and he also decided to study under as many Islamic scholars and mystics as he could. This in turn gave him unique qualifications as a judge, allowing him to find employment in every city and court.

According to his book, *Rihla* (*The Journey*), he took some detours after arriving in Egypt, eventually reaching Mecca via Damascus. Then, he traveled on through Persia, Basrah, and Baghdad to Mongol-controlled central Asia, returned to Mecca for a while, took a trip to East Africa, doubled back to Mecca, then decided to visit India by joining a caravan from Turkey. He ended up visiting the court of the Mongol Golden Horde and claimed to have visited the Crimea and what is now Russia. Then, after joining a court visit to Constantinople, he finally headed back through Asia to Afghanistan and India.

Ibn Battuta, the medieval traveler whose journeys perhaps resembled Sinbad's as closely as could anything in reality. (© Classic Image / Alamy)

In India, he spent a few years working for the Sultan of Delhi, who turned out to be dangerously unstable; Ibn Battuta escaped his court by being sent on a diplomatic mission to China. Unfortunately, he ran into bandits and was delayed for a while in southern India, but he was determined not to report failure, so he traveled on, detouring to the Maldives, where he spent a while as a courtier and chief judge. Still aiming for China, he sailed on via Sri Lanka, only to suffer shipwrecks and pirate attacks. Reaching Sumatra by a tortuous route, he took ship again and reached China via Malaya, Vietnam, and the Philippines. After a stint there, including (he claimed) a visit to Beijing, he finally decided to head home, via India, Basrah, Baghdad, Damascus (where he witnessed the Black Death), Mecca, and Sardinia, coming home after 24 years.

However, he was not quite done with travel; the next year, he volunteered to help defend Muslim Granada from a threatened Christian invasion, then when that proved unnecessary, he turned tourist. A year or two after that, he made a trip to Mali and Timbuktu in West Africa, before finally settling down in Morocco.

Only then did he write his book, or rather dictate it from memory to a professional writer. Not everyone believes every word of it; some descriptions are clearly lifted from older sources, and there are serious discrepancies, especially concerning his supposed visit to Russia; some scholars also doubt that he actually reached China. However, the mere fact that it would have been possible to patch such a tale together, and that people at the time were prepared to treat it as fact, says a lot about the Muslim world of the 14th century.

rig certainly became the standard. It makes ships efficient and maneuverable, but a basic lateen is not very good at tacking, and it can be dangerous to handle in a storm; hence, *dhow* sailors depended on the reliability of the monsoon system. By timing their voyages correctly, they could be sure that the wind would be blowing the way they wanted to go and could usually avoid storms.

Lastly, the earliest *dhows* were almost certainly all "double-ended," coming to a point at bow and stern, but later large designs had square sterns, sometimes highly decorated.

The Navigators

Arab seamen recognized three grades of navigators. The first grade simply knew a set of coastlines and their landmarks and so could be trusted to sail along them, avoiding dangers but not venturing out of sight of land. The second grade could handle journeys across open water, but only by following standard routes direct from one point to another. As the Arabs knew how to determine latitude by observing the stars, this may often have been a matter of staying on the right line of latitude for a given destination. The third and highest grade, the *mu'allim*, was trusted to operate freely out of sight of land, using those stellar navigation techniques and a lot of experience to determine the ship's position.

The Arabs seem to have acquired the magnetic compass from China at some point, and perhaps passed it to Europe during the Crusades. However, it was never used very much in the Indian Ocean.

The captains of the ships on which Sinbad sails seem to be *mu'allim*, as they use mysterious techniques, incomprehensible to everyone else, to determine positions even when well off any known route. However, if they are *mu'allim*, they are often very unlucky; they keep ending up in places where they know they do not want to be.

Trade Goods

Perhaps the biggest reason for all this seafaring was the spice trade. Spices have long been a valuable commodity, and many of them originated in India or points east of there. Growing them elsewhere is often difficult, so they usually had to be transported – by sea, the most efficient means, when possible. In fact, it was a desire to break the Venetian monopoly on the European end of the spice trade that sent the Portuguese into the Indian Ocean in the 15th century. Pepper (from Indonesia) may be the oldest trade-spice, while cloves (from the same area) and cinnamon (from India and Sri Lanka) were also known from ancient times and show up in the stories. Sinbad could have dealt profitably in nutmeg and mace, too; they originate from a few remote islands in Indonesia.

But spices were not the only valuable product available. For example, the original texts mention diamonds and other precious stones, camphor, coconuts, aloes (a family of plants, actually native to Africa, with medical uses), ambergris,

and ivory. Fragrant woods, used in perfumes and incense, were greatly valued in China; agarwood, featured in the story of Sinbad's sixth voyage, is actually a dark, resinous, highly aromatic wood which forms in the trunks of certain tree species when they suffer a mold infection, and comes mostly from southeast Asia, while in Sinbad's time, sandalwood would have come from an Indian species.

For that matter, the relatively ordinary wood from which Arab ships were built was itself quite a valuable resource, as discussed above. Other local trade items included amber, iron and other metals, and palm wine, along of course with supplies of food for the ships' crews and materials used in maintaining their vessels.

Unloading cargo in Oman. To this day, trade on the Indian Ocean sometimes seems little changed from the "Age of Sinbad." (© Marion Kaplan / Alamy)

Sinbad in Later Times

Tales such as those of Sinbad were never intended to remain entirely static. Every medieval coffeehouse storyteller will have told them his own way, perhaps throwing in contemporary references or jokes. Manuscript copies nail them down a little, but anyone reading aloud and innovative or sloppy copyists could introduce changes; printing sets things a little more firmly in place, but then translations bring more subtle changes.

Once Galland introduced them to Europe, the stories began to be adapted to European forms of storytelling, and to be edited to fit European assumptions and sensibilities. They also inspired a long-running fashion for "oriental" stories – part of an 18th-century rebellion against "classical" styles. The strangeness of stories in *The Arabian Nights* was part of their appeal, but western writers were prone to making them sound more like European fairytales, or imposing their own political and racial ideas. And, of course, translators could simply get things wrong, or leave out crucial details.

Sinbad the Legend

By the 19th century, *The Arabian Nights* seem to have been part of the cultural background of every significant writer in Britain and in many other parts of Europe. They were never quite so popular in the United States, but even American literature of the period shows signs of their influence.

Sinbad became part of this; his encounters with giant monsters and strange cultures were classic "travelers' tales," and western readers fell in love with and referenced them. One example is Edgar Allan Poe's "The Thousand-and-Second Tale of Scheherazade" (1850), a supposed epilogue to *The Arabian Nights* in which Scheherazade annoys her husband by telling a story in which Sinbad goes on one last voyage and encounters various "impossible" wonders which had actually been invented by the 19th century.

However, by the end of the Victorian era, *The Arabian Nights* had fallen out of fashion in the literary world. The stories were not forgotten, but they were mostly handed over to children, in safely bowdlerized forms. One setting in which Sinbad remained popular was the Christmas pantomimes which developed in England during that period. The writers were always looking for new plots and names to use, and the Sinbad stories offered exotic

foreign locations (and hence wildly fancy "foreign" costumes), simple plots, shipwrecks and monsters to show off the latest in flashy stage effects, and unfamiliar foreign names to be mangled into bad puns.

Modern and Postmodern Sinbads

The Arabian Nights was were never entirely forgotten by "serious" writers. In fact, their tangled storytelling and complicated history had a definite appeal to modernist authors. For example, James Joyce referenced Sinbad (and a lot else) in novels including his masterpiece *Ulysses* (1922). Likewise, American literary novelist John Barth incorporated such references into several books and essays, culminating in *The Last Voyage of Somebody the Sailor* (1992), an intricate postmodernist novel in which a modern-day American falls overboard from a replica of a medieval ship and somehow washes up in the world of Sinbad and *The Arabian Nights*, where the two men trade stories.

   As a well-known out-of-copyright heroic figure, Sinbad has also shown up in countless children's tales, minor comic books, and other media, as anything from a leading figure to a name to drop.

The Seventh Voyage of Sinbad (1958) is loosely inspired by several parts of the original stories. As the man-eating (two-eyed) giant in one of them is evidently derived from the Greek legend of Odysseus and a one-eyed cyclops, the film features a stop-motion animated cyclops. (© Moviestore collection Ltd / Alamy)

Sinbad Movies

In fact, during the 20th century, Sinbad found a new home, though he
had to take a new form to do it. Hollywood has an omnivorous interest in
heroes, and Sinbad was squeezed into the Hollywood pattern; the stories had
monsters and fantasy wonders to challenge the special effects experts, plus an
excuse for fancy costumes. (Getting starlets into skimpy "harem" outfits was

Patrick Wayne as a sword-fighting Sinbad in *Sinbad and the Eye of the Tiger* (1977). (© United Archives GmbH / Alamy)

often a bonus.) Sinbad movies do not generally follow the original stories very closely; Sinbad is usually transformed from a lucky, resilient merchant into a romantic swashbuckler, and his nickname of "the Sailor" is taken to mean that he's an expert captain, not just a traveler.

Most of the earliest Sinbad movies were short cartoons, but one of the first big Hollywood projects was *Sinbad, the Sailor*, made in 1947, featuring Douglas Fairbanks, Jr., as Sinbad and Maureen O'Hara as his morally ambiguous love interest. This film makes Sinbad a fast-talking rogue on a quest for lost treasure, and it has little in the way of magic or monsters. Other, lower-budget efforts followed this pattern to a greater or lesser extent, but the most famous Sinbad movies were slightly different.

These form a loose trilogy, overseen by stop-motion effects genius Ray Harryhausen: *The Seventh Voyage of Sinbad* (1958), *The Golden Voyage of Sinbad* (1973), and *Sinbad and the Eye of the Tiger* (1977). Harryhausen jumped at the excuse to create a series of fight scenes with weird monsters, a few from the original stories but mostly not, wrapped around with quest plots;

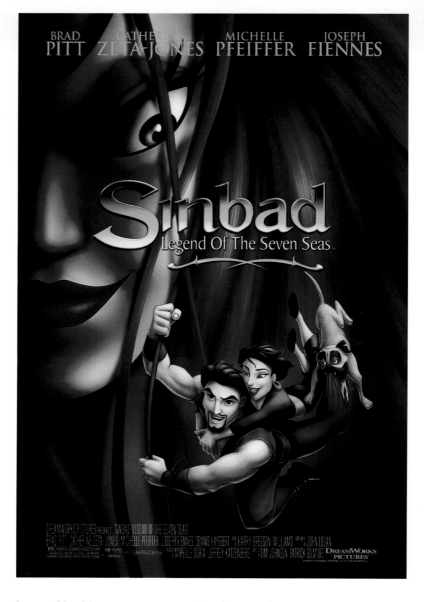

his swashbuckling sea captain was played in turn by Kerwin Matthews, John Philip Law, and Patrick Wayne. Then, in one further twist, Marvel Comics produced comic-book adaptations of two of these movies, and subsequently threw some references to the character into some of their superhero comics, although it is not clear if this is meant to be the same version of the character as in the movies.

Sinbad has also reappeared in animated form occasionally in recent years, notably in 2003 with *Sinbad: Legend of the Seven Seas*, from Dreamworks, with

Brad Pitt voicing the hero, and Catherine Zeta-Jones and Michelle Pfeiffer in support. This draws much more from Greek than Arabian mythology, however, with Sinbad sailing from Syracuse and dealing with the goddess Eris and assorted Greek-style sea monsters and sirens (albeit along with a roc).

Sinbad on the Small Screen

Sinbad has occasionally cropped up in TV productions over the years; one recent appearance was in the British channel Sky1's *Sinbad* (2012), a family fantasy series with lots of computer graphics providing sprawling cities, giant monsters, and the occasional display of sorcery. The series appeared on SyFy in the United States and on the Space network in Canada. Sinbad (Elliot Knight) becomes a youthful rogue and beginner swashbuckler, and even when episodes take ideas from the original stories, they change things around completely. On the other hand, at least the series starts in Basrah, the characters are clearly sailing on a fantasy version of the Indian Ocean, and Sinbad's companions are an attractive multi-ethnic crew.

Unfortunately, though, this was not enough to appeal to modern audiences, and the series was cancelled after one season. Still, it's a safe bet that Sinbad will be back on the screen somewhere, sometime, sooner or later.

GLOSSARY

ambergris: A waxy substance made in the digestive organs of the sperm whale; it was formerly very valuable and was used as a fixative in perfumes.

anecdote: A short account of an interesting or entertaining event.

bowdlerize: To edit a book or other work of art to remove the parts that might offend people.

camphor: A white, waxy, flammable substance with a strong smell; it comes from the East Asian camphor tree.

claimant: A person who claims to have the right to a position, role, or property.

extemporize: To write or perform something on the spot.

formidable: Powerful, large, or skilled enough to inspire fear or respect.

harem: Wives and concubines; the term also means the part of the house in which the wives, concubines, and female relatives of a man lived in a Muslim society.

lateen: A triangular sail set on a long yard that is set at an angle to the mast.

latitude: A measure of how far north or south a location is from the equator.

monopoly: Complete control of a good or service in a particular area.

monsoon: Seasonal winds in the Indian Ocean; they bring heavy rains to southern Asia in the summer.

mystic: A person who seeks knowledge that comes through insight or intuition.

nomadic: Moving around frequently without a fixed home.

oral tradition: Stories and other kinds of cultural knowledge that are passed down by word of mouth.

parable: A short story that teaches a lesson.

porter: A person whose job is to carry baggage or other goods from one place to another.

prohibition: Not allowing something to be present or be done.

puritanical: Very strict, in particular very strict about religion.

rigging: The ropes and lines that are used to control masts, yards, and sails on a ship.

sensibilities: The emotional responses that people have, especially to a work of art.

sheik: An Arabian term for a ruler and leader.

swashbuckling: Brave, dashing, and given to having exciting adventures.

vizier: A high official; the term was historically used in Muslim countries.

FOR MORE INFORMATION

African and Middle Eastern Division
Library of Congress
101 Independence Avenue SE
Thomas Jefferson Building, LJ 220
Washington, DC 20540
(202) 707-7937
Website: http://www.loc.gov/rr/amed/
This division of the national library of the United States has a wealth
of materials relating to the Middle East. Some of these are displayed
in the division's Washington, D.C., online, and traveling exhibitions,
while others can be seen only by contacting the library.

Aga Khan Museum
77 Wynford Drive
Toronto, ON M3C
Canada
(416) 646-4677
Website: https://www.agakhanmuseum.org
This Islamic art and culture museum opened in Toronto in 2014.
Along with a collection of paintings, ceramics, manuscripts, tex-
tiles, and examples of the decorative arts from across the Islamic
world, the museum also features a busy performing arts program.

Bibliothèque nationale de France
Quai François Mauriac
75013 Paris
France
+33 1 53 79 59 59
Website: http://www.bnf.fr/en/tools/a.welcome_to_the_bnf.html
France's national library houses many treasures. Among them is the
Galland manuscript, which is the earliest known edition of *The Ara-
bian Nights*.

International Association for Comparative Mythology
c/o Department of South Asian Studies
Harvard University
1 Bow Street, 3rd Floor
Cambridge, MA 02138
(617) 496-2990
Website: http://www.compmyth.org/
This association studies how mythologies from different areas have
influenced each other and traces the origins of mythologies. The
group hosts annual conferences and encourages the publication of
academic articles on mythology.

Journal of Abbasid Studies
BRILL
2 Liberty Square, 11th Floor
Boston, MA 02109
(617) 263-2323
Website: http://www.brill.com/products/journal/journal-abbasid-
studies
This academic journal publishes articles about the Abbasid Cali-
phate. Authors come from various disciplines, which makes for a
comprehensive discussion of many aspects of the period, including
politics, culture, economics, religion, and intellectual life.

The Metropolitan Museum of Art
1000 5th Avenue
New York, NY 10028
(212) 535-7710
Website: http://www.metmuseum.org
This museum has one of the best collections of Islamic art in the
United States. Visitors can see art from across the Islamic world,
drawn from a period spanning the seventh through nineteenth
centuries. In 2011, the museum reopened its newly renovated gal-
leries for the Art of the Arab Lands, Turkey, Iran, Central Asia, and
Later South Asia.

The Oriental Institute of
The University of Chicago
1155 E 58th Street
Chicago, IL 60637
(773) 702-9514
Website: https://oi.uchicago.edu

Founded in 1919, the Oriental Institute is one of the world's leading centers for the study of Near Eastern civilization. It has sponsored several archaeological digs. Its museum displays objects from its rich collection and hosts special exhibits, such as 2014's Silk Road and Indian Ocean Traders: Connecting China and the Middle East.

WEBSITES

Because of the changing nature of Internet links, Rosen Publishing has developed an online list of websites related to the subject of this book. This site is updated regularly. Please use this link to access this list:

http://www.rosenlinks.com/HERO/Sin

FOR FURTHER
READING

Alpers, Edward A. *The Indian Ocean in World History*. New York, NY: Oxford University Press, 2013.

Ansary, Tamim. *Destiny Disrupted: A History of the World Through Islamic Eyes*. New York, NY: PublicAffairs, 2010.

Bennison, Amira K. *The Great Caliphs: The Golden Age of the 'Abbasid Empire*. New Haven, CT: Yale University Press, 2010.

Bobrick, Benson. *The Caliph's Splendor: Islam and the West in the Golden Age of Baghdad*. New York, NY: Simon & Schuster, 2012.

Gordon, Stewart. *When Asia Was the World: Traveling Merchants, Scholars, Warriors, and Monks Who Created the "Riches of the East."* Boston, MA: Da Capo Press, 2009.

Homer. *The Odyssey of Homer*. Translated by Richmond Lattimore. New York, NY: Harper Perennial Modern Classics, 2007.

Hourani, George. *Arab Seafaring*. Princeton, NJ: Princeton University Press, 1995.

Ibn Battutah. *The Travels of Ibn Battutah*. Edited by Tim Mackintosh-Smith. London, England: Macmillan UK, 2003.

Ibn Fadlan. *Ibn Fadlan and the Land of Darkness: Arab Travellers in the Far North*. Translated by Paul Lunde and Caroline Stones. New York, NY: Penguin Classics, 2012.

Kennedy, Hugh. *When Baghdad Ruled the Muslim World: The Rise and Fall of Islam's Greatest Dynasty*. Boston, MA: Da Capo Press, 2006.

Lyons, Jonathan. *The House of Wisdom: How the Arabs Transformed Western Civilization*. New York, NY: Bloomsbury Press, 2010.

Mackintosh-Smith, Tim. *Travels With a Tangerine: A Journey in the Footnotes of Ibn Battutah*. New York, NY: Random House Trade Paperbacks, 2004.

Mahdi, Muhsin, ed. *The Arabian Nights*. Translated by Husain Haddawy. Deluxe edition. New York, NY: W. W. Norton & Company, 2008.

Mahdi, Muhsin, ed. *Sindbad: And Other Stories from the Arabian Nights*. Translated by Husain Haddawy. New York, NY: W. W. Norton & Company, 2008.

Makdisi, Saree, and Felicity Nussbaum, eds. *The Arabian Nights in Historical Context: Between East and West.* New York, NY: Oxford University Press, 2009.

Paine, Lincoln. *The Sea and Civilization: A Maritime History of the World.* New York, NY: Alfred A. Knopf, 2013.

Sheriff, Abdul. *Dhow Cultures and the Indian Ocean: Cosmopolitanism, Commerce and Islam.* New York, NY: Oxford University Press, 2010.

Touati, Houari. *Islam and Travel in the Middle Ages.* Translated by Lydia G. Cochrane. Chicago, IL: University of Chicago Press, 2010

Villiers, Alan. *Sons of Sindbad.* Reprint edition. London, England: Arabian Publishing, 2010.

Worrall, Simon. *The Lost Dhow: A Discovery from the Maritime Silk Route.* Toronto, ON: Aga Khan Museum, 2015.

INDEX